THOMAS BECKET AND HIS WORLD

Covering one of the most fascinating yet misunderstood periods in history, the MEDIEVAL LIVES series presents medieval people, concepts and events, drawing on political and social history, philosophy, material culture (art, architecture and archaeology) and the history of science. These books are global and wide-ranging in scope, encompassing both Western and non-Western subjects, and span the fifth to the fifteenth centuries, tracing significant developments from the collapse of the Roman Empire onwards.

SERIES EDITOR: Deirdre Jackson

THOMAS BECKET
and His World

MICHAEL STAUNTON

REAKTION BOOKS

Published by Reaktion Books Ltd
Unit 32, Waterside
44–48 Wharf Road
London N1 7UX, UK

www.reaktionbooks.co.uk

First published 2025
Copyright © Michael Staunton 2025

Printed and bound in India by Replika Press Pvt. Ltd

A catalogue record for this book is available from the British Library

ISBN 978 1 83639 070 1

CONTENTS

Martyrdom of Thomas Becket, miniature from an early
13th-century psalter.

Introduction

There is one image of Thomas Becket that is more familiar than any other. We can find it painted in stained glass and depicted in manuscript illuminations, carved into statues, engraved on pilgrim badges, printed in pamphlets and reproduced on book covers. It shows Thomas kneeling or standing, usually before an altar, as a group of armoured knights wield swords above his head. In some versions the violence of the deed is emphasized by the clash of swords and the blood pouring from Thomas's head. Alternatively it is the serene expression of the archbishop as he awaits his fate that captures the attention, or the stately environment of the cathedral in which he is pictured. Sometimes a cross is prominent, held by Thomas, or by a bystander who holds out his arm in an attempt to shield the archbishop from the blow. But in each case it is Thomas's final accomplishment, his violent suffering at the hands of the knights in Canterbury Cathedral, that is presented as his defining moment.

Every attempt to tell the story of Thomas Becket begins under the shadow of his death, but it gains its power from the remarkable nature of the life he led before he faced the knights' swords on the evening of 29 December 1170. Certainly, it was the shocking nature of Thomas's death that prompted crowds of people to stream to Canterbury, to lament his passing and to pray at his tomb. Outrage at the murder of the archbishop of Canterbury in the mother church of England, and the rapidly spreading news of the miracles worked at his tomb, caused Thomas to be hailed as a saint throughout the Christian world, from Iceland to Byzantium. And it was as a martyr of the Church that Thomas's sainthood was officially recognized by the pope within the space of little over two years of his death. But none of this would have happened were it not for the fact that Thomas was already famous, killed at the height of his renown. Bishops, archbishops and even popes had been murdered before, and this was not the first time that murderers had profaned the sanctuary of the church. But Thomas was murdered in his own cathedral in the midst of a clash between the Church and the crown that had divided the kingdom. Not only that, but his murderers claimed to have acted in the name of the king, a man who had raised Thomas first to the position of royal chancellor and then to leader of the English Church, and of whom it was said that he loved Thomas more than his own son.

Those who first began to recount Thomas's story in the immediate aftermath of his murder did so in the face of competing impulses. On the one hand, they wanted to celebrate the life of a man who had, in their minds, been proven to be a saint by the manner of his death and the miracles and acclaim that followed. Therefore, they looked to his earlier life for manifestations of that holiness and greatness that would later be fully realized and revealed, configuring it as a path to martyrdom. But at the same time, they were faced with the fact that Thomas was a tremendously well-known figure, one who had led a very public life for years, first in the royal court and then in the Church. Thomas was controversial and divisive, loved and admired by many, but reviled and detested by others. And perhaps most importantly, Thomas had for much of his life shown few outward signs of the spirituality traditionally expected in a saint. How to reconcile the worldly chancellor, given to hunting and hawking, with the martyr of Canterbury? Many struggled to do so, and it is clear that doubts about Thomas's sanctity, and about his character, lingered after his death. But it is in part because of these difficulties that we are able to gain such a full and nuanced picture of Thomas and the life he led.

We know more about Thomas Becket than we do about any other English person of the Middle Ages. Much of this is because the fascination of his life and death and the events in which he was involved drew so many people to record what they had witnessed, but it is also to do with the world in which he lived. Thomas is one of a number of larger-than-life figures from the twelfth century, the age of Bernard of Clairvaux, Hildegard of Bingen, Eleanor of Aquitaine, Richard the Lionheart and Saladin. These men and women lived at a time of expanding literacy and a new creativity in various forms of writing. They were celebrated in their own day and their deeds were preserved for posterity in letters, diaries, histories, poems and songs. The same is the case for Thomas. Well before his death his secretaries began to collect his correspondence, conscious that they were witnessing historical events that should be preserved for posterity. After his death these letters, numbering more than eight hundred, were arranged in a form that allows us to follow in close detail both the progress of the dispute and the positions of the main protagonists. Within a decade of his death at least ten narrative accounts of Thomas's life and death were written, five of them by witnesses to his murder. Many more would follow, in Latin, French and Icelandic, in prose and verse. At the same time the monks of Canterbury were recording testimony of miracles performed through the martyr's intercession, first at his tomb and in the vicinity of Canterbury but soon all over the Christian world. These volumes comprise the largest medieval collection of miracles of any saint apart from those of the Virgin Mary. And a series of stained-glass windows depicting Thomas's life, death

Reliquary casket of Thomas Becket, Limoges, *c*. 1200, gilt copper alloy, *champlevé* enamel and wood.

and posthumous glory became a centrepiece of Canterbury's newly rebuilt cathedral.[1]

Since the twelfth century Thomas's story has been recognized as an important and dramatic one that demanded to be told and retold. For centuries people have been telling the story in different ways, and this is just the latest attempt to do so. As with any biography, it is both an account and an interpretation. The aim is to narrate some of the most significant events in Thomas's life, as well as his murder and its aftermath, but also to address questions that this life provokes: how did a London merchant's son advance to the position of chancellor to King Henry II, and then archbishop of Canterbury? Did Thomas, as his champions claim, undergo a dramatic conversion on becoming archbishop? Was the rift with his former friend the king based on personal rivalry, or on deeper issues? Was Thomas's murder a willing martyrdom for the Church, or an arrest gone wrong? And how did such a divisive figure become the greatest saint of his age?

The best place to seek answers to these questions is in the numerous twelfth-century testimonies to Thomas's life, written by Thomas himself, his friends, enemies and others. But we may also better understand Thomas Becket if we pay attention to the world in which he lived. For this reason I will often place this life and these events in their broader landscape, looking at the environment that Thomas inhabited: the city of London where he was born, the Church that gave him his first promotion, the developments in kingship, government and law that provided the background to his conflict with the king, the world of politics and ideas in which the dispute was conducted, and the beliefs and practices that prompted his acclaim as a saint. In this way we can see that Thomas was a remarkable figure, but also in certain ways representative of his time. And in turn this eventful life can provide a window into some aspects, at least, of the world of twelfth-century Europe.[2]

Western Europe, detail from the 'Cotton Map', an Anglo-Saxon
map of the world, Canterbury, mid-11th century.

ONE

Thomas of London

Shortly after he was conceived, Thomas's mother is said to have dreamed that the whole River Thames was flowing within her. Frightened at what this strange vision might mean, she went to see a wise man who reassured her that it signalled no danger, but rather, 'the one who is born to you will rule over many people.' Then, on the very day that the child was born, a fire beginning at the family home spread to the neighbouring streets and engulfed their buildings. A little later, when Thomas was still an infant, his mother dreamed that she saw Thomas lying in a cot covered with a precious purple blanket. She and a nurse tried to unfold the cloth, but they found that the room was too small. They went into the hall, and then the street outside, but there was still not enough room to open up the cloth, and when they went out to a field beyond the city walls and tried to unfold it there, they heard a voice from heaven saying, 'It is no use – all England cannot contain it!'[1]

It was customary for such legends, portending a glorious future, to be told about medieval saints, but the stories told about Thomas's birth are especially pointed in that they suggest that he would transcend his origins in a remarkable way. Though born into the relatively ordinary environment of the city of London, his achievements in life and glory in death would bring him a fame that all England could not contain. And whatever about the fanciful nature of the stories themselves, that was something that nobody then or now could deny. Thomas was a commoner who rose to the highest rank in royal administration and then to the highest rank in the English Church, and finally became England's most acclaimed saint, famous all over the Christian world. Thomas's origins set him apart from the large majority of those who held positions of power in the royal court and the higher ranks of the Church, and he was never allowed to forget where he had come from. Right up until his last moments he was reminded by those of more distinguished lineage that he was Thomas Becket, the London merchant's son. But nor was this the simple story of a poor man's rise from obscurity. Though, as Thomas himself acknowledged, he was not 'sprung from noble ancestors', nor were his origins the lowliest.[2] And Thomas was also an example – if an especially striking one – of a phenomenon characteristic of the era. That is, of commoners vaulting over the barricades of social class and advancing to positions of power and influence by virtue of talent and fortune.[3]

The Merchant's Son

In the 1964 film *Becket*, Richard Burton played Thomas Becket as a commoner of Anglo-Saxon blood, facing up against Peter O'Toole's rapacious Norman king, Henry II. In reality, Thomas's family was thoroughly Norman, while Henry II was of mixed Norman, Angevin and Anglo-Saxon descent. Gilbert Becket, Thomas's father, came from the region of Bec in Normandy, the duchy in northwestern France named after the Scandinavians or 'Northmen' who began to settle there in the ninth century. At some stage Gilbert moved to Rouen, Normandy's capital and main commercial centre, on the banks of the River Seine. There he established himself in the textile trade and married a native of the city of Caen named Matilda (or Roheise, by some accounts).[4] There had long been close economic connections over the Channel between Normandy and England. When William duke of Normandy defeated King Harold at Hastings in 1066 and became king of England as well as duke of Normandy, he began the process of replacing the Anglo-Saxon ruling elite with a French-speaking Norman aristocracy. In the early decades of the twelfth century, merchants too were migrating in increasing numbers from Normandy to London, among them Gilbert and Matilda. They must have been well settled in London by the time Matilda gave birth to a son on the feast of St Thomas the Apostle, 21 December 1120 (or possibly 1118).[5]

In the century after his death a romantic legend grew up around Thomas's parentage. An English knight named Gilbert Becket went on crusade to the Holy Land, only to be captured by a powerful Muslim emir and imprisoned in his castle. There, goes the legend, Gilbert won the heart of the emir's daughter, who helped him to escape from prison and return to England, but not before she had extracted a promise from him that on his return he would send for her and marry her. After some time, she embarked on the perilous journey to England, knowing only two words to help her in her search for her husband-to-be, 'Becket' and 'London'. They were reunited, she was baptized a Christian and the couple married in St Paul's Cathedral. Gilbert made another pilgrimage to Jerusalem, and on his return found that his wife had given birth to a son, Thomas.[6] Though there is no historical basis to 'the Saracen legend', it is clear why it was told: the story of descent from an emir's daughter provided Thomas with noble blood. Indeed, similar stories were often told of crusaders of apparently humble background who made a name for themselves in the Holy Land. For whereas noble blood certainly did not guarantee greatness, in the twelfth century an illustrious life that lacked an illustrious birth could be hard to explain.

A more persistent legend concerns Thomas's name. Though he is still sometimes referred to today as Thomas à Becket, he was never called that in the Middle Ages, and this designation likely originated in a confusion with Thomas à Kempis, author of popular devotional books in the fifteenth century. The meaning of 'Becket' is not quite clear either, but it has been suggested that it derives from Gilbert's origins near Bec, or even his 'beaky' nose.[7] In any case, Thomas was likely known as Thomas of London when he was younger, before becoming Thomas the Chancellor, Archbishop Thomas and St Thomas of Canterbury.

Thomas grew up right in the heart of London. Today the Mercers' Hall stands on the site of the Becket family home, tucked between Ironmonger Lane and Old Jewry, just off Cheapside. Cheapside takes its name from the Old English *ceape* or market, and in the twelfth century it was one of London's principal food markets, a relatively broad street lined with stalls. The names of many of the narrower streets leading into Cheapside recall the produce sold there: Honey Lane, Bread Street, Milk Street, Poultry. These were the food markets that sustained London's population of 20,000 or more, more than twice that of any other English city. But the names of the adjoining streets illustrate the trades that gave London its purpose: Wood Street, Staining Lane, Cannon Street (formerly Candle-wright Street), as well as Ironmonger Lane where Thomas was born. On the other side of Thomas's birthplace is Old Jewry, in Thomas's time simply The Jewry. London's first Jewish community had come from Rouen, drawn by the establishment of Norman rule in England. Though they were under the special protection of the king, and allowed their own synagogue and law court, they were generally restricted from involvement in other trades beyond finance and money-lending, and they were subject to the king's whim. In 1290 King Edward I would expel all Jews from England, and from

then on the street adjoining Thomas's birthplace became Old
Jewry, a relic of a lost community.

Towering over the street where Thomas was born stood two
familiar London landmarks, symbolic of the two institutions
that Thomas would serve later in life. To the east, by the river,
stood the Tower of London, begun in the reign of William the
Conqueror, its square keep of gleaming white limestone from
Caen in Normandy a constant reminder of the dominance of
England's new rulers. To the west stood St Paul's Cathedral –
not the building that stands today, but an even larger and more
imposing stone building, begun in 1087 and destroyed in the
Great Fire of London in 1666. In Thomas's day it was the most
distinguished of over a hundred churches in London and its
surrounding area. It would also in time come to be the seat of
Thomas's sharpest critic, the bishop of London, Gilbert Foliot.

Thomas was not born into poverty. By 1120 Gilbert Becket
had amassed substantial wealth in the textiles trade, and later

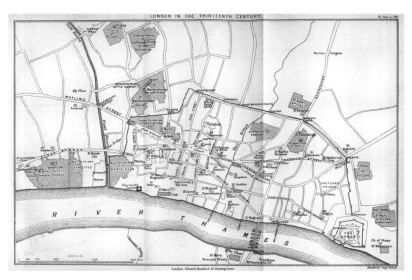

London in the 13th century, map from W. J. Loftie, *A History of London*,
vol. 1 (1883).

through income from properties. The family home seems to have been a substantial one, and Gilbert belonged to the city's merchant elite, even serving a term as sheriff of London. A few details survive about Thomas's mother, Matilda, too. She is described as a devout woman, who inculcated the faith in Thomas, and in particular a devotion to the Virgin Mary. It is said that when Thomas was an infant she would put him on weighing scales, balanced against bread, meat, clothes and money, and she would then distribute his weight in these alms to the poor.[8] Thomas also had at least three sisters: Mary, who would become a nun at Barking Abbey in Essex and later its abbess, Agnes, who went on to found St Thomas's Hospital, and a third sister Roheise.[9]

It was in the twelfth century that people first began to write of the glories of London, one contemporary claiming that 'the only plagues of London are the immoderate drinking of fools and the frequency of fires.'[10] But it was still in many ways a dangerous and difficult place to live. In the words of another twelfth-century writer, 'Whatever evil or malicious thing that can be found in any part of the world, you will find it in that one city.'[11] Thomas, growing up in a prosperous family, would have been protected from many of such perils. Matilda probably initiated her son's education in basic Latin, reading and writing, and then when he was about ten years old he was sent away to be educated at Merton Priory in Surrey.[12] This was a house of Augustinian canons, men who lived according to a rule similar to monks but less isolated from worldly affairs. Thomas seems to have retained an affection for Merton, and in later years Prior Robert of Merton would act as his private confessor.

At some point Thomas returned to London to study in one or more of the grammar schools. Though neither Thomas nor any of his schoolfriends left behind reminiscences of his youth in the schools of London, we have a priceless contemporary insight into the life he might have led. William fitz Stephen, a

Londoner, was chaplain and secretary to Thomas when he was royal chancellor and continued in this position when he became archbishop. After his death fitz Stephen wrote a lively and informative *Life of St Thomas*, which begins with a description of the city in which both he and Thomas were born.[13] He pays particular attention to the schools of London, describing how the boys of different schools would hold public debates, darting abuse and gibes at each other, bantering in epigram and rhythm, as the audience guffawed and applauded.[14] He also pays much attention to the sports of the city, saying that 'it is not fitting that a city should be merely useful and serious-minded, unless it be also pleasant and cheerful.'[15] He describes the annual carnival day when scholars from the different schools would bring fighting-cocks to do battle. In what is thought to be the earliest description of football, he writes,

> After dinner all the young men of the town go out into the fields in the suburbs to play ball. The scholars of the various schools have their own ball, and almost all of the followers of each occupation have theirs also. The seniors and the fathers and the wealthy magnates of the city come on horseback to watch the contests of the younger generation, and in their turn recover their lost youth.[16]

Different seasons meant different types of games. Every Sunday in Lent the young men would go out to the fields on warhorses and play at war games, the younger ones with the steel points of their lances removed. At Easter youths would hurtle down the river current in small boats attempting to strike a lance against a shield fixed to a tree. If they missed, they were thrown overboard and fished out downstream in sight of the laughing spectators. Throughout the summer the young men play at archery, running, jumping, wrestling, slinging stones, throwing javelins, and fighting with sword and buckler. At night the maidens dance 'and until the moon rises, the earth is shaken with flying feet'. In winter hounds are let loose to fight with bulls, bears or boars. And when the great marsh beyond the city's north wall was frozen over, swarms of young men pour out of the city to play on the ice, using poles and skates make from animal bones. The result is often cuts and broken limbs, but, says fitz Stephen, 'Theirs is an age greedy of glory, youth yearns for victory.'[17]

The impression one gets is that Thomas was more enthusiastic about such sports than he might have been about study. None of his biographers say much about his qualities as a student, or any enthusiasm for learning, but all agree that from an early age he took an interest in hunting with horse and hounds, a passion that lasted well into adulthood. While he was attending school in London, Thomas spent much of his time at the home of a family friend named Richer de l'Aigle, a wealthy nobleman who initiated Thomas in such aristocratic pastimes. On one of their outings when Thomas was following Richer across a narrow bridge, the boy's horse slipped and fell into the fast-flowing river below. Dragged by the current towards a millwheel, Thomas seemed sure to be crushed by it, except that the mill-keeper, entirely ignorant of the boy in the water, decided at that moment to close off the water from the mill, thereby saving him. Or rather, as Thomas's biographers saw it, divine mercy miraculously saved the boy, preserving him to be a future leader of the Church.[18]

An Uncertain Start

There were two main paths to greatness for someone born in England in the early twelfth century, and one of those was closed off to Thomas. Commentators of the time liked to think of their society as strictly ordered, with everyone in their proper place. They spoke of those who worked, those who fought and those who prayed. This meant (and here they really meant male society) a division into the rural peasantry, the landed military aristocracy and the clergy. As a broad categorization this made sense, but it left out certain groups, including that to which Thomas belonged, a group that was on the rise but whose status remained undefined. Though wealthy, Thomas's family did not have the resources that inherited land conferred on those of noble birth, or the social cachet that came with distinguished blood. And although his father was an influential figure in London society, Thomas did not benefit directly from the patronage of the king as senior nobles did.

There was, however, another route to advancement that was beginning to open up just at the time that Thomas was growing to adulthood. This was advancement through administrative service. In Thomas's time it was becoming increasingly common for young men of non-noble status to enter the service of a king, an important lay lord or a senior ecclesiastic, and from there to work their way up to positions of wealth and influence. One of the great historians of the early twelfth century, Orderic Vitalis, dismissed them as 'men raised from the dust', and others were disturbed that men of low birth were being placed in positions of influence.[19] It was not social engineering but rather the practical demands of the time that caused their rise. Powerful men in various aspects of life – kings, senior ecclesiastics, nobles, businessmen – were increasingly reliant on letter-writing, accounting tasks, record-keeping and administration, and they turned to men who were literate and numerate. In early twelfth-century England such men comprised a small but growing number, and they were as likely to be found among commoners of Thomas's rank as among the lower nobility. Innovations in bureaucracy demanded a new type of servant to staff bureaucracies that could look after their lands, finances, entourages, legal cases and communications. For a young man like Thomas, the usual path to such service and advancement was education. But if that did not go as planned, then connections and luck might also work.

When he had finished his schooling in England, around the year 1140, Thomas went to Paris to study.[20] It was an exciting time to be there. The University of Paris would not yet emerge for some decades, when the various independent schools in the city formed into the large-scale, self-regulating institution that we call the university. But already these schools were attracting students from all over Europe to study the liberal arts, or to advance to higher studies such as theology. This was where Peter Abelard had recently taught, scandalizing opinion by his original approach to philosophical and theological problems as much as by his affair with his student, Heloise. He was succeeded by less controversial but perhaps more influential teachers, such as Hugh of St Victor and Peter Lombard. Paris was right at the centre of the revival of classical learning, and the flourishing of new intellectual, scientific, literary and religious perspectives to which modern historians have given the name 'The Twelfth-Century Renaissance'.[21] But if they affected Thomas Becket in any way, we have little evidence of it.

Thomas's biographers say little about his time in Paris. One suspects that he did not distinguish himself, but perhaps also his career as a student was derailed by circumstances beyond his control. Gilbert Becket suffered a series of losses from fires and ended up bankrupt, with almost all his property destroyed. The son of the wealthy merchant now found himself with neither aristocratic blood nor wealth, heir to nothing, carrying the stigma of financial and social failure. More devastating was the death of his mother to whom he was devoted, when he was twenty-one. Thomas abandoned his studies in Paris and returned to London. Soon after, unable to bear living there without his mother, he chose to move out of the family home, though without any clear idea of what to do.[22] We are told by one of his biographers that he spent his 22nd year without definite employment. It was, however, but a momentary pause before Thomas the Londoner would take his first step on the ladder that led to power, riches and a fame that would spread far beyond the city of his birth.

There survives a description by an anonymous contemporary of Thomas's appearance at this time, just before he began his advance through the ranks:

> He was then twenty-two years of age, a slim man of pale
> countenance and dark hair, with a large nose and regular
> features. He was gentle of manner and sharp of intellect,
> and he was easy going and amiable in conversation.
> He was authoritative in speech, if somewhat stammering.
> He was so keen in discernment and comprehension that he
> would always solve difficult questions wisely. His memory
> was so amazing that whatever he heard of scriptures and
> legal judgements he was able to cite at any time he chose.
> On account of God's gifts that have been mentioned, wise
> men could easily see that he was predestined to a great
> position in God's church.[23]

William fitz Stephen gives a similar picture, describing the young man as

> Handsome and of pleasing countenance, tall of stature,
> with a prominent and slightly aquiline nose, nimble and
> active in his movements, gifted with eloquence of speech
> and an acute intelligence, high-spirited, ever pursuing
> the path of virtue, amiable to all men, compassionate
> towards the poor and the oppressed, but hostile to the
> proud, zealous for the promotion of his fellows, not from
> any insincerity, but out of pure courtesy and kindness,

for he was intent on securing the respect of all good
men. He was liberal and witty, ever on his guard against
deceiving men or being deceived by them, at once
a prudent son of this world and destined to become
a child of light.[24]

In both accounts, Thomas's illustrious destiny seems self-evident,
even at such a young age. But as a description of a saint, there
is something tentative about these impressions of Thomas's
youthful merits. Saints were often described in childhood and
adolescence as 'adding virtue to virtue' and 'growing in favour
before God and man', but the qualities identified in the young
Thomas are markedly worldly in character. Herbert of Bosham,
a man who came to know Thomas better than any of his other
companions, later wrote that when Thomas reached adulthood,
he threw away discipline and abandoned those lessons that he
had learned at school. Amusing himself with horses and hounds,
he filled his days with vain and trivial pursuits: he 'fed on the
winds and followed shadows'.[25] Reflecting on Thomas's youthful character, Herbert writes that some are gifted with urbanity:
they are worldly, sociable and pleasing to those around them,
if not necessarily good and pleasing to God. Others are gifted
with goodness, making them more solemn and austere, pleasing
to God rather than men. It is best, he says, for those who lead
a public life to combine both, to be all things to all men, while
also pleasing God. In the first years of his adulthood, he says,
Thomas excelled in the former grace, but lacked true goodness:
'He advanced in age and grew in attention and favour with men
but not so with God.' But, he says, God later gave him that other
grace of goodness, so that he might advance likewise before men
and God.[26]

In many ways, then, Thomas's early life was undistinguished,
especially for one who would later be hailed as England's greatest

saint. Indeed, Thomas's posthumous biographers had difficulty in portraying those early years. Not only was first-hand witness less easily available than it was for his later, more public exploits, but Thomas's early life was in some ways an embarrassment. Before he became archbishop of Canterbury in his forties, Thomas showed little solemnity and less austerity. Instead, after a shaky start, he became a very successful careerist and a social climber.

But even while acknowledging the worldliness of Thomas's early career, his later advocates could identify traits that marked him out as a man of God, and which laid the foundations of his later identity. They claimed that his religious purpose was nascent from an early age, waiting for the right moment to emerge. And, as Herbert of Bosham put it, those who receive gifts of grace late should be seen as just as worthy as those who receive them early.[27]

A Career in Administration

Thomas's first employment was in the city of London, though there is some dispute as to the nature of his job. Some accounts have him serving a man named Osbert Huitdeniers ('Eightpence'), a relative and a man of property and of high standing. It seems that Osbert was a moneylender and Thomas was employed managing his books.[28] Another source suggests instead that Thomas served the municipal authorities of London as a clerk and acted as accountant to London's sheriff.[29] He may have done both. Little information survives on this, his first employment, though one detail is intriguing. It is said that Thomas was inclined to join in with the lewd conversation of the other boys, so as not to appear different from them, while within his mind was on higher things.[30] Already we have a glimpse of one of Thomas's most remarked-upon characteristics, his ability to be 'all things to all men' while at the same time concealing his true purpose.

Whatever his precise occupation it is clear that for these three years Thomas was a clerk. The Latin word *clericus* has given us in English the word 'clerk' and also the word 'cleric', and in the twelfth century their meanings overlapped. A clerk – someone who was educated and literate – was usually in religious orders; and those in religious orders tended to be literate and educated. The word 'clerk' was usually applied to those in minor religious orders, distinguished from the rest of society by their modest dress and their hair, cut at the top of the head in a tonsure. They were meant to avoid taverns and tournaments, and were not allowed to carry weapons, but they were not necessarily ordained, and they were allowed to marry.[31] Thomas may already have been in minor orders when he was working for Eightpence, and before long he fully embraced a career in the Church. Working for a relative in the city of London was beneficial for a young man whose grief at the death of his mother and distress at his father's declining fortunes might otherwise have left him rudderless. But real advancement lay in the Church, and soon Thomas had his big break.

Some of Thomas's biographers suggest that he made a deliberate decision to enter the service of a great churchman: that he wished to defend the honour of the clergy against oppression by the nobility, and considered a career in the Church to be more fitting than one in the secular world.[32] But this is a projection back from his later advocacy on behalf of ecclesiastical rights, and it is more likely that Gilbert saw an opportunity for advancement for his son. By an important quirk of fate, Theobald of Bec, the new archbishop of Canterbury, consecrated in 1139, came from the same region of Normandy as Gilbert Becket. We are told that Gilbert often conversed with Theobald about the region and their families, and it appears that mutual acquaintances arranged for a more formal introduction of Thomas to the archbishop.[33] Theobald, impressed by the young man, invited him to join his household.[34]

Canterbury, for its part, must have made an impression on Thomas. For five and a half centuries the church of Canterbury had been England's most important and powerful ecclesiastical see, playing a central role in the country's religious, political, intellectual and cultural life. The Gothic cathedral that stands today did not exist in Thomas's day – it originated in the decades after his death – but the building that he entered in the early 1140s was itself an impressive stone structure, 30 metres (100 ft) in width. This was the seat of the archbishop of Canterbury, who exercised jurisdiction over twelve diocesan bishops, and claimed primacy over England's one other archbishop, the archbishop of York. Although in most of Europe cathedrals were staffed by canons, the church of Canterbury was staffed by monks, around 150 of them in Thomas's time. The monastic community of Christ Church, Canterbury, was a venerable one noted for its learning and its library. Conforming to a jealously guarded tradition, Archbishop Theobald himself was a monk.[35]

Thomas and the other clerks lived in the same complex of buildings as the monks and they had much interaction with them, but the archbishop's household was different in character in many respects.[36] The monks lived a life devoted to poverty, chastity and obedience, guided by the sixth-century Rule of St Benedict, which ordered every aspect of their life, from prayers to food to sleep. The archbishop's household was staffed by remarkably talented and ambitious men, of noble birth and well educated. Many of these other clerks would, like Thomas, advance to high ecclesiastical office. Thomas soon prospered, impressing the archbishop with his prudent advice, his energy and his faithful service, and within a short period of time he was promoted to his inner circle of advisors. This, it seems, provoked a backlash from some of his colleagues. It is said that one of these, Roger of Pont l'Évêque, himself part of Theobald's inner circle and holding the position of archdeacon of Canterbury, was so

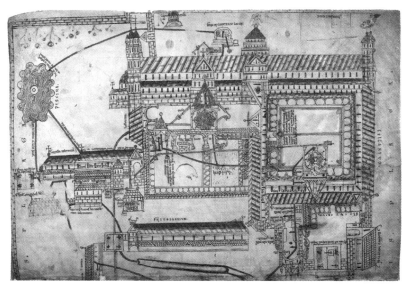

Plan of Canterbury Cathedral, from the *Eadwine Psalter*, 12th century.

jealous of Thomas that he let it spill out in insults and taunts, calling him 'Baillehache's clerk' after the man who had introduced him to court.[37] 'Baillehache', meaning 'Carry-Axe', seems to have been Theobald's marshal, in charge of horses and stables, and presumably a family friend.[38] This is one of the many reminders that Thomas was given as he advanced in his career of his relatively humble origins, but it is also a sign of how easily Thomas could make enemies. Roger would go on to be archbishop of York and would play an important role in Thomas's later life, and in his death.

As one of the archbishop's leading advisors and administrators, Thomas held an important and varied role. The archbishop was a man of many parts. He was the head of the monastic community, its *abbot*, though the day-to-day running of the monastery was left to the prior. He was a *prelate*, governing the diocese of Canterbury, which extended over most of the county of Kent. He was also a *metropolitan*: as archbishop he had authority over the province of Canterbury, that is, the dioceses of the southern part of England and their bishops; the archbishop of York governed the smaller northern province. And finally, he was – though the archbishop of York often disagreed – primate of all England, the leader of the English Church, the main link with the king and the pope. Thomas's first duties were to look after the archbishop and his estates and to govern the diocese. The diocese of Canterbury was relatively small, but it was rich. By 1066 almost a quarter of the land of Kent belonged to the Church, and Canterbury had also accumulated huge estates beyond Kent, in Berkshire, Oxfordshire and elsewhere, as grants from rich nobles. The archbishop was, then, a major landlord, with responsibilities for castles and knights. Thomas helped to administer these estates, collecting rents and overseeing properties, whether by accompanying the archbishop on his rounds of his manors, or by writing letters on his behalf.

But Theobald also broadened the young clerk's horizons, sending him away to study law for a year at Bologna in Lombardy and then some time in Auxerre in Burgundy.[39] The archbishop had his own courts, where he presided as judge, and a mass of judicial material passed through his writing-office. Knowledge of the law was crucial to the defence of Canterbury's rights against encroachment from other ecclesiastics, from lay magnates, or from the king. Fitz Stephen tells us that Thomas studied civil and canon law, and Bologna was the acknowledged centre for both.[40] In the second half of the eleventh century scholars at Bologna rediscovered Justinian's *Corpus Iuris Civilis* (Body of Civil Law), a sixth-century compendium of laws and legal opinions based on centuries of Roman legal tradition. They began to apply to their own society not only individual laws that had lain dormant for centuries, but Roman principles of civil law. This systematic approach was also applied to canon law – the law of the Church. Canons are rules of right behaviour and derive

from various sources: the Bible, the writings of early Christian
authorities such as St Augustine and St Ambrose, decrees of
early Church councils, papal letters and other materials. Canon
law had long existed, but it was only at the turn of the twelfth
century that it began to be codified in a coherent way, and it
found its most influential expression in the compilation known
as Gratian's *Decretum*. Thomas is never credited as being much
of a scholar, but in his time at Bologna and Auxerre he must
have picked up not only some formal legal training, but a sense
of the importance of the law to the Church and its rights.[41]

Fitz Stephen also tells us that Theobald on several occasions
sent Thomas to Rome on business, and there 'he conducted
himself prudently and was accorded high favour by the pope
and the holy Roman church.'[42] One of these matters of business
concerned Canterbury's status as the head of the English Church.
Canterbury's position was – in the eyes of the archbishop and
community at least – pre-eminent within England. When Pope
Gregory I ('the Great') sent a mission in 596 to convert the
English, it was welcomed by King Aethelberht of Kent, who converted to Christianity and allowed the leader of the mission,
Augustine, to establish his see at Canterbury. Subsequent archbishops of Canterbury asserted their authority over the whole
English Church, but although its history, its wealth and its strategic position between London and the main Channel ports
gave Canterbury great importance, it had to defend its primacy
against challenges from other churches and ecclesiastics. During
Theobald's early years as archbishop he had to contend with
the rival authority of Henry of Blois, bishop of Winchester and
brother of King Stephen, who had been appointed by Pope
Innocent II as his legate in England. This made Bishop Henry
the pope's representative, with powers to summon Church councils, decide major cases and influence ecclesiastical elections.
When Henry's appointment lapsed on the pope's death, Thomas

played an important part in lobbying Rome to have Theobald made legate, efforts that bore fruit in 1150. But more important for his own future and for the future of the kingdom of England was Thomas's involvement in the succession to the throne. To explain how this came about we must go back some time, to the year of Thomas's birth.

A New King

On 25 November 1120, a month before Thomas was born, a fleet of ships disembarked from the Norman port of Barfleur to make the short journey across the Channel to England. One of these ships carried King Henry i. The youngest legitimate son of William the Conqueror, Henry had succeeded to the throne when his brother King William ii 'Rufus' was killed by a stray arrow while hunting in the New Forest in 1100. Henry saw off the challenge from his brother Robert 'Curthose', duke of Normandy, defeating him in battle and incarcerating him for the rest of his life. In 1120 King Henry was at the height of his power, governing England and Normandy with a firm hand, aided by innovations in administration and law. But as Henry was crossing the Channel another craft, known as the *White Ship*, ran aground and sank, taking with it some of the cream of the English nobility, including Henry's seventeen-year-old son and heir, William. When King Henry died in 1135 without a legitimate male heir, a succession crisis ensued. The late king had designated his daughter Matilda as successor and demanded an oath from his leading vassals to recognize his will. They did so, but reluctantly. Not only had no woman succeeded to the throne of England before, but Matilda had spent much of her life outside the realm, married first to the emperor of Germany and on his death to Geoffrey Plantagenet, count of Anjou, the Normans' aggressive and acquisitive neighbour. So when, in 1135, King

Henry's nephew, Stephen of Blois, claimed that the king had changed his mind on his deathbed and chosen him instead, there were many willing to believe him.[43]

But if Stephen's actions in seizing the throne showed initiative and drive, these qualities appeared sorely lacking in him thereafter. He never managed to stamp his authority on the kingdom, giving away too many concessions to his rivals at one time, taking disproportionate action against important friends at another. By 1139 Matilda and her half-brother Robert of Gloucester were in open rebellion. In 1141 their forces even captured King Stephen, but they threw away their advantage, failing to achieve the necessary recognition for Matilda's succession, and allowing Robert to be captured by forces loyal to the king. By the late 1140s, when Thomas was in Archbishop Theobald's service, the conflict was at a stalemate. Matilda, unable to dislodge Stephen from the throne, retreated to Normandy where she and her husband Geoffrey gradually took control of the duchy. Stephen had survived as king but never regained full control over his kingdom, which remained subject to outbreaks of rebellion, conflicts among barons and families, and pillaging by private armies and foreign mercenaries. 'Every man built himself castles, and filled them all with devils,' as one chronicler put it, and in these days 'Christ and his saints slept.'[44] It was only with the emergence of a credible new candidate for the throne that this period, which historians have termed 'the Anarchy', would come to an end.[45]

In 1133 Matilda gave birth to her first son, whom she named Henry after her father. The boy grew up in Anjou, Normandy and England in the separate courts of his father Geoffrey Plantagenet, his mother Matilda and his uncle Robert earl of Gloucester. From an early age he was surrounded by knights and mercenaries, and gained a training in arms and horsemanship, but he was also educated in courtesy and how to speak and

Effigies of Eleanor of Aquitaine and Henry II, Royal Abbey of Fontevraud, early 13th century.

read Latin. His determination to take up his mother's cause was demonstrated at the age of fourteen when he led a small force of knights into England against Stephen. Though soon forced to retreat, the young Henry would in time show himself to be a more formidable opponent. Knighted at the age of sixteen, he began to take an active part in the defence and governance of Normandy, and in 1150 his father Geoffrey resigned the duchy into his son's hands. Soon after this, Geoffrey died, leaving Henry both duke of Normandy and successor to his father's Angevin lands.[46]

Then Henry took advantage of a crisis in the French kingdom. King Louis VII of France and his wife Eleanor of Aquitaine had for some time become estranged on account of both personal differences and the failure to produce male heirs, and their marriage was annulled in 1152. Eleanor did not have to wait long for a new husband. Renowned for her intelligence and beauty, she was also heiress to the lands of Aquitaine, comprising the large part of southern France. Eight weeks after the dissolution of her marriage, she married Henry, about eleven years her junior, in a hastily arranged ceremony at Poitiers.[47] It was a transformative coup for the young duke of Normandy and count of Anjou, Maine and Touraine in the north, who now found himself in addition the lord of Poitou, Saintonge, Périgord, Limousin, Angoumois and Gascony in the south. But his full inheritance remained to be taken. In January 1153 Henry landed with a fleet of 36 ships and a large force near Bristol. Soon many of the greatest magnates gave their support to the challenger, and King Stephen was forced to come to terms. In November 1153 it was agreed that Stephen would remain king for life, but Henry would succeed him. The new heir to the throne returned to Normandy, and it was there that he received the news nearly a year later that King Stephen had died unexpectedly on 25 October, and that England awaited its new king.

Henry's succession was widely welcomed among the leading powers of England, not least within the Church, weary of the violence, disorder and instability that had characterized his predecessor's reign. Archbishop Theobald had clashed with Stephen a number of times. In 1148 he had disobeyed the king's prohibition on attending a papal council at Rheims in France, dashing to the coast and crossing the Channel in a small boat, with one companion, his clerk Thomas.[48] Again in 1151, when Stephen sought to secure the succession of his son Eustace to the throne, Theobald sent Thomas to Rome to secure a papal prohibition on such a coronation. Then in 1153 it was Archbishop Theobald, with other leading ecclesiastics, who initiated the compromise between Stephen and Henry Plantagenet over the English throne. In these negotiations Theobald was again assisted by his trusted advisor, Thomas of London, and it was perhaps on

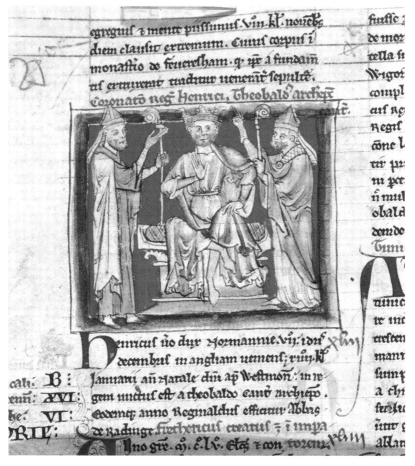

Coronation of Henry II, miniature from Matthew Paris, *Flores Historiarum*, 1250–52.

this occasion that the future king of England first encountered the archbishop's clerk.[49]

By now Thomas was a man of some importance, having met many of the most influential figures in the Church and gained experience of politics at the highest level. He had also become rich. As rewards for his efforts, he had over the years accumulated churches of his own, and the revenues that accrued from them.

Then in the summer of 1154 his rival Roger of Pont-l'Évêque was appointed archbishop of York, and Thomas took over his position of archdeacon, second-in-command to the archbishop. But his career was soon about to take a different direction. As England prepared for the arrival of its new king, the archbishop of Canterbury took on the role of regent, and it is likely that much of the business of the realm was in the hands of his archdeacon. Henry landed on 8 December and was crowned king by Archbishop Theobald on 19 December. Soon after this he chose as his chancellor the man who had worked so effectively in securing his succession. Thomas, the careerist clerk, would now find himself in a position that brought unimaginable fame, riches and power, but would put to the test all his natural resources of prudence and intelligence. He would discover that not even he could remain all things to all men.

TWO

Royal Chancellor

Even if he had never progressed any further in his career, had never become the controversial archbishop or the martyr of Canterbury, Thomas Becket would have had a place in the history of medieval England. For Thomas was the king's right-hand man at a time of extraordinary change in the kingdom of England. This was a time when strong royal government was restored after the Anarchy of King Stephen's reign (1135–54), when the power of the king was extended over his subjects as never before, and when the administrative state and the English Common Law came to be firmly established. In all this Thomas was not only an active and loyal servant of the crown, the king's effective representative, administrator and counsellor, but he became his companion in work and play. So much so that, as one contemporary wrote, 'Never in Christian times were there two greater friends, more of one mind.'[1]

Thomas's able execution of his duties and his friendship with the king made him a figure of great significance in the kingdom, but this became a problematic legacy for Thomas when he later sought to present himself as a champion of the Church. As critical churchmen noted, Thomas had seldom shown himself to be a friend of the priesthood while he was chancellor, and his status as the king's minister and ally cast a cloud of suspicion over his appointment as archbishop. Another matter was the chancellor's conspicuous worldliness. As Thomas would later himself confess, he had been devoted to hunting and hawking and other secular pursuits and had become accustomed to dressing in fine clothes and dining lavishly. It should not be surprising, then, that after Thomas's death, the archbishop's supporters made some effort to explain these years in the king's court. Some claimed, not entirely convincingly, that already as royal chancellor Thomas was making strenuous behind-the-scenes efforts on behalf of the Church. Others acknowledged fully the contrast between the worldly chancellor and the holy archbishop and martyr, stressing the transformation that occurred on his appointment as archbishop. But whether friends or critics, all would appreciate the significance of Thomas's time as the king's man.

In the King's Service

According to William fitz Stephen, the early days of the new king and new chancellor saw the dawning of a glorious new age after nearly two decades of darkness. During Stephen's reign, he writes, some barons built unlicensed castles as their bases, other nobles were disinherited, and foreign mercenaries and violent men roamed over the country. It seemed to many that the kingdom could never be returned to its former dignity and peace, especially with such a young king. But with the advice of the chancellor and the support of the clergy and nobles of the realm, mercenaries were expelled, castles built without royal licence were surrendered or destroyed, and the crown of England was restored after its decline: ancient rights were returned to the disinherited, and all rejoiced in peace. Swords were beaten into ploughshares, lances into scythes. The Church was honoured, and the king, with God's favour, prospered in all his doings: 'The realm of England was enriched, the horn of plenty was filled to the brim. The hills were cultivated, the valleys abounded in corn, the pastures with cattle and the folds with sheep.'[2]

If this seems overblown, it also happens to be supported in its main elements by other evidence. Upon becoming king, Henry held his first Christmas court, and there he issued a charter in which he confirmed 'all the concessions and gifts and liberties and free customs that King Henry my grandfather gave and conceded to them. Likewise, all evil customs that he wiped out and remitted I remit and concede that they be wiped out by me and my heirs.'[3] This is the kind of language we find again and again in Henry II's official documents: references to 'the time of my grandfather' and the 'evil customs which have sprung up since that time'. Stephen's reign had been declared an aberrant interlude, and royal authority reasserted. Not only that, but the new king made that assertion a reality. When some of the more powerful – whether old enemies of the Angevins or former allies – insisted on their independence and defied the king, Henry immediately challenged them, marching against them and using force if necessary. Soon other barons, seeing that they were dealing with quite a different king to Stephen, surrendered their castles or fled the country.[4]

Henry's achievement in pacifying the kingdom is testimony to the vigour of his own personal rule, to which contemporaries attest. Sketches have come down to us from clerks who worked

Reverse of the royal seal of Henry II depicting the king on horseback, 12th century.

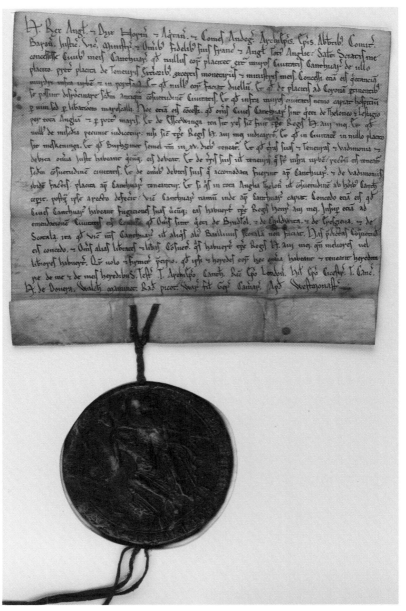

Charter of Henry II to the City of Canterbury, 1155–61, ink on
parchment, with the seal of Henry II depicting the king enthroned.

in his administration of his appearance and character, and they give us a picture of a young man bursting with vigour, at once simple in habits and extraordinary in his labours. Of medium height, with a round head, red hair and a leonine face, his eyes are described as white and plain when calm, but when angry shining like fire and flashing in fury. 'Curved legs, a horseman's shins, a broad chest, and a boxer's arms all announce him as a man strong, agile and bold.' Most striking is his energy. He is described as constantly on his feet from morning to evening, whether at conferences or at Mass or in any other business, only sitting to eat or when on horseback. He wore simple clothes, and was devoted to hunting, always occupying himself with some exercise so as not to let his flesh weigh him down. He could be both fascinating and terrifying. As one writer put it, this was 'a man whom men flocked to gaze upon, though they had scrutinized him a thousand times already'.[5] But one of Henry's greatest achievements was to recognize that he could not rule by personal charisma and energy alone. Indeed, perhaps the most lasting legacy of his reign is his establishment of an administrative and legal structure that would cause the English to be among the most efficiently and closely governed people of the time.

What was the chancellor, and why did this position make Thomas Becket such an important figure in the kingdom? This is what fitz Stephen says:

> The chancellor of England is considered second in rank in the realm only to the king. He holds the other part of the king's seal, with which he seals his own orders. He has responsibility and care of the king's chapel, and maintains whatever vacant archbishoprics, bishoprics, abbacies and baronies which fall into the king's hands. He attends all the king's councils to which he does not even require a

summons. All documents are sealed by his clerks, the royal seal-keepers, and everything is carried out according to his advice.[6]

There may be some exaggeration of the historical importance of the chancellorship here, but it is nonetheless a broadly accurate picture of the chancellor's role when it was held by Thomas. The chancellor was originally the king's chaplain, in charge of the royal chapel which followed the king as he travelled around his lands, and responsible for church services at court. It was, then, in its origins a domestic office, one among many others in the king' s household – the marshal, the steward, the butler, the chamberlain, the treasurer – who looked after the king's everyday needs. But by the time Thomas was appointed the chancellor's role had gained a new importance, and the reason for this lies in the broader transformation of royal government.

Henry II was noted by contemporaries for his energetic personal rule, traversing great distances to ensure the loyalty of his senior vassals, to browbeat his ministers and to cow his enemies. But personal rule could only achieve so much when a king's lands stretched from the North Sea to the Pyrenees. Since 1066 a permanent bureaucracy had been developing at Westminster just outside London's city walls. It thrived under King Henry I, who raised talented men from obscurity to serve in his administration. At Westminster there emerged systematic practices that served to channel the king's resources and tighten his hold over his subjects, and the technology they used was writing. This is what made the chancellorship so important: the scriptorium, or writing-office, was originally a subsidiary of the royal chapel, and so, as the writing-office expanded, the office of the chancellor grew in importance.

Henry II and his chancellor were not, of course, the first to introduce writing to royal government. Long before the Norman

Conquest, kings of England had issued written instructions to their local representatives and granted or confirmed privileges in writing to religious houses and other beneficiaries. What was new in the twelfth century was that such practices became far more frequent, so that official communications in writing became commonplace, and claims to lands or other rights increasingly required written authority. These trends were already apparent in Henry I's reign but were impeded by the disorder and weakness of King Stephen's rule. Henry II's determination to return to the strong royal government of his grandfather manifested itself not only in direct challenges to disobedient vassals, but in a desire to rebuild and expand the bureaucracy that Henry I's policies had encouraged. In his reign we can see the volume of written documentation multiply, an immediate sign of how royal government becomes more centralized and systematized.[7]

Thomas was at the centre of this administration, and he played a variety of other roles in the king's government. He was a baron of the exchequer – that is, one of the men responsible for the audit of the king's finances. The exchequer takes its name from a table at Westminster, covered in a chequered tablecloth, around which the justiciar, the chancellor, the treasurer and other senior royal officers met twice a year, at Easter and Michaelmas. These men examined the accounts of the king's sheriffs who managed the royal estates, taxes and individual debts. In order to calculate what needed to be paid in and out of the royal treasury, counters were moved up and down the chequered tablecloth as if on a chessboard. The exchequer is first recorded during the reign of Henry I and is the earliest central financial office in Western Europe. It might seem a very rudimentary system of financial oversight, and a distinctly unglamorous example of the assertion of royal power, but in fact it served far-reaching purposes. This was recognized by Richard FitzNeal, a member of King Henry's household who wrote a manual on the working of this system,

called *The Dialogue of the Exchequer*. There he writes, 'Abundance
of means, or the lack of them, exalts or humbles the power of
princes. For those who lack them will be a prey to their enemies,
to those who have them their enemies will fall a prey.' Kingdoms
are ruled through virtue, but what is conceived with sound counsel
needs to be carried through by what Richard calls 'a routine-like
method'. It is such a routine method of maintaining royal finances, he says, that allows for towns to be fortified and soldiers
to be paid, for churches to be built and for the poor to be fed and
clothed.[8]

At this time, too, Thomas occasionally acted as a judge on
the king's behalf. During his chancellorship the system of royal
courts and standardized practices that would come to be known
as the 'English Common Law' was in its infancy, but in the following decades these judicial reforms would grow in pace and would
stand as one of the most important legacies of Henry II's reign. We
can see the results of this revolution in royal administration,
finance and law today in Westminster as the seat of government
of the United Kingdom, in the office of Chancellor of the
Exchequer, the head of His Majesty's Treasury, and in the legal
system that prevails over much of the English-speaking world.

Officers receiving and weighing coins at the exchequer,
detail of miniature from the *Eadwine Psalter*, 12th century.

None of these innovations originated entirely with Henry II, but in each case he gave them renewed and lasting impetus. His motives were far from solely altruistic: in each case they brought tangible benefits to the crown. As we will see, the dispute between Henry II and Thomas Becket was founded at least in part on the pressure that the expansion of royal authority, as facilitated by such institutions of government, placed on the Church. And although Thomas was often willing to embrace elevated rhetoric about the superiority of ecclesiastical over royal authority, his time as chancellor showed him the importance of such mundane matters as bureaucracy, finance and law to the pursuit of his aims.

The Courtier

These are some of the formal duties of the chancellor: he was the head of the chancery, a baron of the exchequer, and also on occasions acted as a judge on the king's behalf. But this tells only part of the story. During these years Thomas was also a member of the king's court. The court is so hard a concept to define that one of its number in Henry II's day wrote, 'In the court I exist and of the court I speak, and what the court is, God knows, I know not.'[9] The court was not a place. Rather, it constituted those people who had access to the king, whether at the seat of royal government at Westminster or at one of the king's residences throughout his realm. Membership of the king's court was ever changing, as some came into the king's favour and others drifted away from it. But throughout his time as chancellor Thomas remained one of those closest to the king. This also meant that throughout this time Thomas was surrounded by other courtiers – either men of high birth or men of ambition and talent like himself who had achieved a position in the king's government. In such an environment, Thomas began in his mid-thirties to soak up the culture of the court – its politicking and intrigues, its sports and pastimes, its wealth and display. It was a culture that Thomas would take to with enthusiasm, and here again fitz Stephen is our witness and guide.

He tells us that the chancellor's house and table were open to the needs of any visitors to the king's court, and hardly a day did he dine without counts and barons as guests. Thomas ordered his floors to be covered daily with new straw or hay in the winter, fresh bulrushes or leaves in the summer, so that the multitude of knights, who could not all fit on stalls, could find a clean and pleasant space, and leave their precious clothes and beautiful shirts unsoiled. His house shone with gold and silver vases, and abounded in precious food and drink, so that if a certain food was known for its rarity, no price would deter his ministers from buying it. Aristocrats from England and further afield placed their children in the chancellor's service, and he provided for them, along with their attendants, teachers and servants. Most notable among these young men in his service was the king's eldest son and heir, also called Henry, who would later play a significant role in Thomas's last days. Thomas, says fitz Stephen, was famous for his generosity, every day giving away horses, birds, clothes, gold or silver wares or money. He carried on his love of field sports too, hunting with dogs and with hawks and falcons, and he also played chess – a noble game that like hunting was regarded as a simulation of warfare.[10]

The most striking picture of Thomas's new magnificence and extravagance is found in fitz Stephen's account of the chancellor's embassy to Paris in 1158. The purpose of the embassy was to confirm the betrothal of King Henry's son Henry to Margaret, daughter of King Louis of France. No matter that Henry was not yet four years of age, and Margaret just a few months old, this betrothal was designed to reinforce the peace recently made by the two kings over the disputed Norman frontier. Such embassies customarily provided an opportunity to exhibit the

wealth and munificence of the petitioner, but Thomas's out-
landish display surpassed all expectations. The chancellor took
the road to Paris with a household of about two hundred knights,
stewards, servants and sons of noblemen, along with their own
attendants, all arranged in appropriate order, horses, wagons,
dogs and birds and supplies of every kind. All were dressed in
glistening new clothes, while the chancellor himself came with
twenty-four changes of clothing, many garments of silk, elegant
cloths, foreign pelts and tapestries, almost all intended as gifts.
There were eight wagons, each drawn by five sturdy horses. Two
of these wagons carried just ale, while others carried various kinds
of food, vessels and ornaments of the chapel, money, books and
furnishings, including everything from precious goblets to basins,
salt cellars and fruit bowls. Each wagon was attended by smartly
dressed grooms and dogs, and on top of each horse sat either a
long-tailed monkey or an ape. As the procession of footservants,
wagons, horses, knights and clerks clattered over the paving
stones of the French villages and towns, the locals would rush
out of their houses to ask whose retinue this was. And when they
were told that this was the chancellor of the king of England on
a mission to the king of France they said, 'If this is the chancellor,
what must the king be like!'[11]

The relationship between Thomas and Henry was more
than that between a trusted servant and his lord. As fitz Stephen
presents it, and this is borne out by others, theirs was marked
by a deep bond of friendship. Indeed, part of the reason why the
role of chancellor became so elevated during Thomas's tenure
was because of this personal bond. The king, says fitz Stephen,
often dined at the chancellor's house, on some occasions purely
for sport, at other times to see for himself what he had heard
about his house and table. Sometimes the king came riding on
horseback into the house while the chancellor was sitting at
table, perhaps with an arrow in his hand, coming from a hunt

or on his way there. He might have a drink and leave when he
had met with the chancellor, but at other times he would leap
over the table and sit down to eat. When important business had
been dealt with, the chancellor and the king would play together
like young boys of the same age, in the hall, in church, in court
and out riding. He tells the story of how the king and his chancellor were riding through the streets of London one day in
bitter winter weather when they saw a poor old man approaching,
wearing flimsy rags. Agreeing that it would be a worthy deed to

King John hunting a stag with hounds, miniature from *Liber legum
antiquorum regum* (The Book of the Laws of Ancient Kings), *c.* 1321.

present the pauper with a warm heavy cape, they fell to debating over which of them should do it, until Henry suddenly grabbed at Thomas's cape, saying, 'To be sure, this great act of charity will be yours!' King and chancellor wrestled with each other strenuously, almost falling off their horses as Henry tried to seize Thomas's cape and Thomas resisted. Finally, the chancellor gave in and, to great laughter, the poor man was presented with the warm cape and walked away, pleased and bemused.[12]

The Chancellor at War

It is easy to forget, among the hawks and hounds, the expensive plates of Parisian eels and the boisterous play with the king, that Thomas remained a man of the Church throughout his time as a king's minister. As chancellor he looked after the king's chapel, and he also retained his position as archdeacon of Canterbury. Archbishop Theobald had recommended his clerk for the position in the hope that he would restrain King Henry in his dealings with the Church,[13] and some of Thomas's biographers claim that he did indeed have a positive influence on the king. Fitz Stephen notes that Thomas would not allow the king to keep Church offices vacant (thereby retaining their revenues), but insisted that they be filled with men of good reputation. Thomas completed the building work on his former place of education, Merton Priory, and provided for it financially, and he also helped to soothe potential conflicts between the king and certain ecclesiastics.[14] Another of Thomas's clerks, John of Salisbury, later wrote that Thomas was so exhausted by the weight of the chancellor's business, and by the deceits of other courtiers, that he would sometimes say that he despaired of living. Although, John says, the world seemed to flatter and applaud him, the chancellor did not forget his clerical status. Seeking to balance his duties to the king with those to the

Church, he often had to act like Proteus, the shape-shifting figure from Greek mythology, administering business while at the same time being engaged in a righteous struggle.[15] As another biographer wrote, 'How he played the part of the double man, the man of the Church and the man of the court, is not easy to explain.'[16]

Some suggest that outward excess hid inner virtue. Despite the luxury of his table, Thomas would provide rich alms for the poor. Amid secular glories he often received discipline in secret, his back stripped for whipping by religious friends. The story is told of how Avice of Stafford, a beautiful woman said to be the king's mistress, would send gifts to Thomas every time he visited her town. The rumour spread that they were having an affair, and Thomas's innkeeper, curious to find out, crept into the chancellor's room at the dead of night and found his bed empty. Assuming that Thomas had gone to Avice's house, he began to leave when his lamp fell on Thomas, prostrate on the ground, having fallen asleep from repeated prayers and genuflections. So, comments one biographer, a religious man was found, where a sensualist had been sought, showing how easily we may judge a man not knowing what is in the man.[17] But such accounts are retrospective ones, written down in the light of Thomas's murder and popular acclaim, and even his biographers concede that when Thomas became chancellor he leaned equally to trifles and serious things. Embracing the clever talk of the court, writes William of Canterbury, he looked for glory, and was 'charmed by the popular breeze'.[18] Another biographer, Edward Grim, attests to Thomas's importance in court, his splendour and wealth, his faithfulness to the king and the honour that the king gave him in return. But alas, he says, for a wicked world! The more a man grows in worldly power, the more prone he is to sin; the richer he is, the loftier his position, the greater the danger of ruin.[19]

Claims of hidden asceticism are hard to verify, but it is easier to form a judgement on Thomas's outward actions as chancellor, and here we can identify certain ways in which Thomas acted to the detriment of the Church or, at the very least, colluded with the king in neglecting its interests. The most glaring example is the Toulouse campaign of 1159. King Henry's lands in France extended from Normandy, inherited from his mother, and Anjou, Maine and Touraine, inherited from his father, to the southern lands of Aquitaine, gained through his marriage to Eleanor. Legally, King Henry held these lands from the king of France. That is, in France (but not outside of France) King Louis VII was Henry's overlord, and he was Louis's vassal, owing homage, allegiance and such services as the supply of troops in time of war. But in effect King Louis's centre of power was in the north-central part of his kingdom, the Île-de-France, and beyond that region he lacked the strength and authority to demand fulfilment of Henry's feudal obligations. But nor was Henry entirely free to ignore the wishes of the French king, as his campaign of 1159 demonstrated.[20]

On Henry's southeastern frontier lay the county of Toulouse, prized for its access to the River Rhône and the Mediterranean Sea. The dukes of Aquitaine had long laid claim to it, and when Louis was married to Eleanor of Aquitaine he too had made aggressive moves in her name. Now that claim had passed to Henry, and in 1159 he made elaborate plans to put it into action, preparing a campaign to take Toulouse for himself. Many of Thomas's biographers point to the chancellor's importance in the venture, and John of Salisbury identifies him as the architect of the whole project. The Toulouse adventure involved the largest mobilization of troops yet in King Henry's reign. The army was led by his most prominent vassals from across his domains, and even included King Malcolm of Scotland. These magnates brought their own troops with them, and Thomas too provided seven hundred choice knights from his household. But the army also required the service of paid mercenaries, and here the king called on a recently introduced method for raising funds, an aid known as scutage (literally 'shield-money'), a cash payment in lieu of military service owed by his chief vassals. To the consternation of ecclesiastics, who had previously been exempt, they too were made liable for this payment, and some laid the blame specifically on the chancellor for initiating this unheard-of burden on the Church. Some years later Bishop Gilbert of London would remind Thomas, now archbishop, of how he had plunged a sword into the bowels of the Church.[21]

In June 1159 this great force moved south from Poitou and advanced on Toulouse, but the adventure would be thwarted by King Louis who raced south with a light force and managed to enter the city of Toulouse. Against a large, well-prepared army, he had played his trump card – his suzerainty over Henry, who now faced the choice of storming the city that held his overlord or withdrawing with humiliation. The chancellor, we are told, was adamant that the city should be attacked, arguing that Louis had abdicated his position as lord by violating treaties and standing against the king of England. But Henry, reluctant to attack the city in which his lord was installed, retreated. Though a humiliation, it is easy to see Henry's rationale. Toulouse, though a great prize, was not worth the possible consequences of attacking his lord. A great lord himself, with many vassals in diverse places, he must have considered how his own vassals might behave towards him. He also might have remembered Thomas's apparent disregard for such bonds in later years.

Thomas's opportunity to display his military prowess was not lost, however. When Henry returned north, he left behind his chancellor along with the constable Henry of Essex to protect the neighbouring castles they had captured on their advance. Fitz Stephen writes,

And later the chancellor put on hauberk and helmet and
with his men took three heavily fortified castles which
seemed impregnable. He also crossed the Garonne with
his troop of soldiers in pursuit of the enemy, and when
all this province had been confirmed in obedience to the
king, he returned in favour and honour.[22]

Thomas took to the battlefield again a year later. In the autumn
of 1160 King Louis's wife Constance died in childbirth and he
promptly married Adela, of the house of Blois. Horrified by this
marriage alliance, and the threat that it might pose to his south-
western flank, King Henry responded with a marriage of his own.
Taking advantage of the presence of visiting cardinals, he swiftly
gained ecclesiastical dispensation for his son Henry to be married to Louis's daughter Margaret. And so the wedding, arranged
with such elaborate pomp by Thomas a few years before, was
joined with great haste. Henry followed this up by seizing
Margaret's promised dowry, lands on the Norman frontier.
Thomas led an army comprising seven hundred knights of his
own household as well as 1,200 hired cavalry and 4,000 infan-
try. 'Although he was a clerk,' writes fitz Stephen, 'he fought
on a spurred horse set at a gallop with lance lowered, with a
strong French knight from that region, Engelram of Trie, and
succeeded in knocking him off his horse and claiming his
charger.' The chancellor's knights were always first in the battle,
always the most daring and most excellent. And even though
the chancellor ravaged the land with fire and sword, his out-
standing faithfulness and nobility impressed the French king
and all the French magnates, 'for virtue may be praised even in
an enemy'.[23]

   Not everyone, however, expressed such unreserved praise
for Thomas's wartime record. His biographer Edward Grim
writes:

Who can number on how many he inflicted death and
confiscation of property? Surrounded by a strong body
of knights, he attacked whole states, destroyed cities
and towns, gave villas and estates to the greedy flames
without one glance of pity, and showed himself merciless
to the enemies of his lord in whatever quarter they arose.
Finally, whom did he ever fear to offend in order to satisfy
the desires of the king or to obey his commands?[24]

Another figure who would express concern about Thomas the
chancellor was the man who had facilitated his appointment,
Archbishop Theobald. While Thomas was assisting the king in
administration, diplomacy and war, Theobald was declining into
infirmity. There survives a letter, astonishing in its frankness,
from the archbishop to Thomas, urging him to return from the
king's side across the sea to visit him:

You have now been recalled again and again to your post,
you who ought to have returned at the first summons of
your old and aging father. Indeed it is to be feared that the
Lord may punish your delay, if you still turn a deaf ear to
my appeal, forgetful of all my kindness and regardless of
the father whom you ought to have borne upon your
shoulders in his sickness.[25]

But the chancellor ignored his pleas, and Theobald died on
18 April 1161, at the end of a long and distinguished career, but
one that would ultimately be overshadowed by that of his
successor.

Although the see of Canterbury took a year to be filled, it
seems that Thomas's name immediately came to be noised about
as a candidate. William fitz Stephen tells us that Thomas was
recovering from an (unspecified) illness at the monastery of

St Gervase, Rouen, when he was visited by Asketil, prior of Leicester, who was on his way back from King Henry's court in the south of France. The prior found the chancellor sitting at the chess table, dressed in a hooded cape. 'Why are you wearing a cape with long sleeves?', he asked. 'This dress is more fitting to a falconer.' He reminded Thomas that, though chancellor, he remained an ecclesiastic with many dignities, 'and, according to the rumour repeated around court, a future archbishop'. Thomas replied,

> I know three poor priests in England, any of whom
> I would choose for promotion to the archiepiscopate
> before me. For if it happened that I were promoted,
> inevitably I would either lose the king's favour or
> (far be it!) neglect the Lord God's service, for I know
> my lord king inside out.[26]

Herbert of Bosham tells a similar story. When the news of Theobald's death was spread abroad, the court was full of speculation that the chancellor would succeed, but Thomas had no confirmation of Henry's intentions until he called on the king at his castle of Falaise. There Henry called him aside and told him that he wished him to be archbishop of Canterbury, to which Thomas, pointing with a smile at the florid clothes he was wearing, said,

> What a religious, what a saintly a man you wish to appoint
> to such a holy see and above such a renowned and holy
> community of monks! I know most certainly that if by
> God's arrangement it should happen, very quickly you
> would turn your heart and favour, which is now great
> between us, away from me, and replace it with the most
> savage hatred. I know for sure that you would demand a

great deal, and even now you are very presumptuous in ecclesiastical matters, which I would not be able to tolerate easily. And so the envious would take advantage of the opportunity, and once favour is extinguished they would stir up endless hatred between us.[27]

A New Archbishop

Canon law had clear specifications as to what type of man should be appointed to high office in the Church. 'Before a bishop is ordained,' read the canons of Gratian, 'he should be examined to see if he is by nature wise, peaceable, temperate, chaste, sober, careful in his business, friendly, merciful, lettered, learned in God's law, skilful in interpreting scripture, well versed in church teaching.'[28] On the evidence of his own biographers, and on his own admission, Thomas would have struggled to meet many of these standards. But in reality there were other qualities expected of an archbishop of Canterbury that reflected less the canonical ideal than the demands of the various interests that he would serve. The first of those interests was the king, and for Henry II Thomas's suitability was obvious. His practical ability and energy were self-evident, he had experience in both ecclesiastical and secular affairs, and his loyalty seemed secure. Most of all, Henry must have considered that Thomas would be the ideal partner in carrying out his ambitions. One specific ambition was to secure the recognition of his eldest son as heir to the throne, and to have him crowned king during his own lifetime. But also, from Henry's point of view, a major area of the business of the realm remained to be addressed: the relationship between the crown and the Church. With the chancellor's help, the first eight years of his reign had seen him carry out extensive reforms that had re-established the authority of the king, both symbolically and in practical terms. Lands and privileges that had been lost to powerful nobles during Stephen's reign were restored to the king. Administrative, financial and legal innovations had helped to establish the necessities of the crown on a firmer footing and extended the reach of the king's authority over his subjects. Yet the freedoms that the Church had become used to had remained mostly untouched while Archbishop Theobald was alive. Now Henry was presented with an opportunity to reshape the relationship between the crown and the Church in a way that fitted into his broader plan of reform and restoration.

This is not to say that King Henry expected Thomas to acquiesce unquestioningly in his ambitions. Thomas would be aware of his distinguished predecessors, the respect due to the traditions of the church of Canterbury, and the necessity of pleasing the monastic community of Christ Church, Canterbury. As the leader of the English Church, Thomas would need to listen to the divergent views of the English episcopate. He would also need to defer to the wishes and authority of the pope and the Roman Church, to which the English Church in the preceding decades had become increasingly bound through ties of bureaucracy, communication and law. And, of course, Thomas himself was a churchman who owed his first promotion to his predecessor, Archbishop Theobald. Yet Henry could be reasonably confident that his relationship with Thomas would be of one type rather than another. He could look to the examples of Archbishop Dunstan, who worked hand in hand with King Edgar in the late tenth century to reform the English Church, or Archbishop Lanfranc, who acted as a partner to King William I in managing the changes to the kingdom and the Church that followed the Conquest. Such archbishops were pious men, and not averse to criticizing kings when necessary, but a good working relationship between archbishops and kings was more the norm than the exception.

Archbishop Theobald had been installed by King Stephen as a way of blocking the ambitions of his brother, Henry of Blois, bishop of Winchester. But Theobald's two predecessors, Ralph d'Escures and William of Corbeil, had been messier appointments, compromises between the wishes of the monks of Canterbury and the bishops. King Henry made sure that there would be no such problems this time. In principle, the monks of Canterbury had a free voice in the election of their archbishop. This was important to them for practical reasons. The man appointed archbishop automatically became their abbot, and the monks wished their ancient right to election to be respected and, if at all possible, to assert the tradition that the archbishop of Canterbury should be a monk himself. In this case, the king upheld the principle of free election, but made it clear that the monks were free to choose any candidate only as long as it was the chancellor. He sent to Canterbury his justiciar, Richard de Luci, who urged the monks to choose someone 'who is equal to such a burden, worthy of the honour and pleasing to the king' and warned them that should they choose someone less pleasing to the king, they would find only division and discord. It is reported that some monks complained that it would be improper to appoint a man who was not a monk, or in another version, to place a follower of hounds and hawks in charge of a flock of sheep.[29] Nonetheless, any objections were overcome, and the monks acclaimed the chancellor as their new archbishop.

The next step was for the election to be ratified more widely, and to this end the senior clergy, lay nobility and royal officials were summoned to a great gathering at Westminster on 23 May 1162. It is unlikely that all present were happy about the nomination. Just as King Henry hoped that Thomas would carry through his reforms, many of the English bishops would have feared for the liberty of the Church with the appointment of the king's right-hand man. But in the end, only one voice was raised publicly against it – that of Gilbert Foliot, bishop of Hereford and soon to be bishop of London, of whom we will hear much more. Whatever Gilbert's objection was, he was persuaded to accept the nomination, and Thomas was unanimously elected.[30]

What were Thomas's feelings about all this? There were real reasons why he might have been wary of such an appointment. John of Salisbury, in a passage echoed by many writers, tells us that Thomas well understood the morals of the king and the wicked pertinacity of his officials, and he concluded that should he take on the office he would inevitably lose either God's favour or the king's. For a time he resisted his election, until the papal legate Henry of Pisa persuaded him to accept.[31] If Thomas did initially refuse the office, it was nothing out of the ordinary – indeed one could say it was standard behaviour. His predecessor Anselm was so reluctant to accept his appointment that he had to be dragged forcibly to the archiepiscopal throne with the bishops pressing the staff into his hand as he struggled and cried out against it. In fact, an anonymous biographer of Thomas lists various examples of ecclesiastics and saints who had initially resisted high office before reluctantly accepting in deference to God and worldly superiors, adding that many at the time considered that the chancellor was by no means reluctant enough.[32]

The new archbishop elect now made his way from London to Canterbury where he was due to be consecrated in great state. Among his retinue was his clerk Herbert of Bosham, who tells us that as they were travelling along the road to Canterbury, Thomas sent for him, and confidentially revealed to him a dream that he had the night before in which he was offered ten talents – obviously a reference to the gospel parable in which the man who invested his five talents and gained a further five was told, 'Well done, good and faithful servant; thou hast been faithful over a few things, I will make thee ruler over many things.' Then

Thomas urged a task on his clerk. 'This is my instruction to you,' he said. 'Whatever men say about me, you tell me boldly but in private. And if I fail in any of my work, as I say, I want you to tell me freely and confidently, but secretly.' Many things, Thomas explained, would now be said about him behind his back, and he asked Herbert to bring to his attention anything he should notice, 'For four eyes certainly see better than two.'[33] Though an archdeacon, Thomas was not yet a priest, and so on 2 June he was ordained at Canterbury. And the following day he was consecrated archbishop in the cathedral by Henry, bishop of Winchester, before a great crowd of bishops, monks, clergy and people, including the leading lords of the kingdom. Though he was greeted with remarkable exultation, Thomas's biographers say that the new archbishop proceeded with great humility and contrition, tears copiously flowing, thinking more of the burden than the honour.[34] There was also, it seems, an ominous moment in the proceedings. It was customary for the newly consecrated archbishop to have a copy of the gospels held above his head and for him to point at random to a passage which would act as his 'prognostic', a foreshadowing of his term in office. To the horror of those present, Thomas's finger pointed to the mysterious story in the gospel in which Christ cursed a barren fig tree with the words, 'May no fruit ever come from you again!'[35]

But this is not mentioned by any of Thomas's biographers, who instead saw it as a moment of glorious transformation. According to Herbert, a change had already begun to come upon Thomas as soon as he had been elected as archbishop. Like a man awaking from a deep sleep, he says, Thomas considered in his heart what he had been for a long time, and how he ought to be from now on. Over the years at court he had been forgetful of himself, but now he began to return to himself and meditate in his heart, and in this meditation his heart grew warm and soon began to kindle a flame. Now, he says, the 'new man', who

had been hidden in the habit of the 'old man', began to be nour-
ished and strengthened and hungered to be revealed.[36] Others
point instead to his consecration as the moment that ushered
in his transformation. William fitz Stephen tells us that anointed
with the holy oil, 'he put off the old worldly man, and put on
Jesus Christ.' Now Thomas, 'contrary to the expectation of the
king and everyone else, so utterly abandoned the world and so
suddenly experienced that conversion, which is the finger of
God, that all men were astonished at it'.[37]

Henry II and Thomas Becket arguing, miniature from *Chronicle of England*, c. 1307–27.

THREE

Conversion and Conflict

There is something that everyone agrees about Thomas Becket: that he experienced a notable change upon becoming archbishop. To those who looked back on his life as that of a saint, this was a moment of conversion, in which he was touched by the hand of God, and the old man was transformed into a new man. And even those more sceptical about Thomas's sanctity could see that something remarkable had happened to change the king's loyal servant into the head-strong champion of the Church's liberties. But if it is agreed that Thomas changed, there has always been disagreement as to what this change meant. To his supporters, Thomas's defence of the Church and apparently newfound spirituality uncovered something that had always been there but was hidden. To his critics, Thomas never succeeded in putting off the proud and worldly chancellor. How can we, at hundreds of years distance, make a judgement on what is described as a change of heart, hidden even to most contemporaries? And how can we understand the way Thomas changed from the king's servant to the Church's standard-bearer?

Many modern theories have been advanced as to Thomas's change of heart. Some have seen his turn to a more spiritual life as little more than self-seeking posturing. Others have identi-fied a genuine change that was proved by his bravery in death. Another influential suggestion is that Thomas was like an actor adept at fulfilling whatever role presented itself. We may never fully understand what caused Thomas to change on becoming archbishop, and what exactly this change involved, but we can appreciate it better if we put the claims of Thomas's biographers in the context of contemporary attitudes towards conversion. This shows us that the conversion claimed for Thomas was not a single dramatic rupture with the past, but rather the beginning of a process of change that would be fulfilled in his death. Another important point is that, although Thomas surprised many by the way in which he began to uphold zealously the rights of the Church, his actions were precipitated not only by his own, apparently new, attitude to ecclesiastical liberties, but by King Henry II's actions in relation to the Church. Although Thomas's own actions are often the focus of attention, in many respects he was responding to the king's initiative. The king

Pilgrim badge from the shrine of Thomas Becket at Canterbury Cathedral depicting his reliquary bust, early 15th century, lead alloy.

was introducing measures that might have caused tensions with any archbishop. They demanded a response, and it is the nature of Thomas's response that caused tensions to explode into a full-blown crisis.

A New Life

Thomas's change of life is clearly presented as a conversion. The language used – touched by the 'hand of God', putting off the 'old man' and putting on the 'new man' – is biblical and is commonly used in medieval saints' Lives to depict a moment of conversion. But there are important aspects of Thomas's transformation, as it is presented, that have caused people to question whether this constituted a true conversion. First, in Thomas's case, change appeared to be an entirely inward phenomenon, hidden from others, at least in his early years as archbishop. There was no flash of lightning or fall from a horse as St Paul experienced on the road to Damascus. Thomas did not cast off his possessions in the public square, as Francis of Assisi would do some decades later.[1] In fact, it seems that in his early days as archbishop, there were complaints that he had not changed sufficiently. There was, as we have seen, some reluctance among the monks of Canterbury to appoint a non-monastic monk, and now Thomas faced complaints that he was entering the cathedral choir in clerical dress. One of Thomas's clerks reported to his master that a man of terrifying countenance had appeared to him in a dream, commanding him, 'Go tell the chancellor to change his garb straightaway, because if he fails to do so, I shall go against him all the days of his life.'[2] Edward Grim says that Thomas began to dwell on how he had squandered his life on transient worldly glories. He realized that if he was to tend to the flock that had been committed to him, he must despise earthly things, and so he 'declared war on himself'. That is, he decided to punish the body and to conform to the life of a monk – but inwardly, not outwardly.[3] Similarly, William of Canterbury writes that Thomas set out to renew the old man. Thinking about how high he had climbed, and how previously as a courtier he had neglected himself, he exerted himself to make up for lost time. So, 'as if transformed into another man', Thomas became more restrained, more watchful, more frequent in prayer, more attentive in preaching.[4]

As an expression of this inward transformation, Thomas began to adopt a threefold manner of dress. On the outside, he continued to wear the garb of a canon and archbishop, thereby retaining to observers his apparent secularity and magnificence. But beneath that, he secretly adopted the monastic habit, so that he could conform to the life of his brothers, though without them knowing. Not only that but underneath, close to his skin, Thomas began to wear a hairshirt of rough cloth that covered his body right down to his shins and swarmed with lice and vermin. In this way Thomas emulated the ascetics of the early Church, men such as St Anthony who retreated to the desert, subjecting the body to the spirit. As William of Canterbury puts it, 'within [Thomas] subdued the illicit stirrings of the flesh, suffering the hardships of the desert without being in the desert'. Quoting the words of the Roman writer Seneca, William fitz Stephen writes, 'His outward visage was like that of ordinary men, but within all was different.' He was like St Sebastian who outwardly fought as a soldier in the Roman army, but inwardly fought as a soldier of Christ, or St Cecilia, who wore a hairshirt under her precious marriage dress.[5]

This is one of the most famous images of Thomas: the outwardly magnificent archbishop humbly subduing the flesh in a monastic habit and hairshirt. But is it believable? Many historians have considered it to be a posthumous fabrication, prompted by the lack of compelling evidence otherwise of an inner spirituality. Others have argued that Thomas may well have been wearing the monastic habit and hairshirt on the day that he died, but that this did not date back to his consecration.[6] The wearing of a hairshirt was not unknown among medieval saints, and the biographers are unanimous in confidently attesting to it. Some writers cite witnesses to Thomas's habit of concealing his true asceticism and piety. Alan of Tewkesbury describes how a monk laughed at the archbishop for apparently putting on weight, not realizing that it was the bulk of the hairshirt and habit that gave the false impression.[7] Fitz Stephen cited the personal testimony of Thomas's confessor, Robert of Merton, that he always remained chaste.[8] On the other hand, this is the most difficult of all claims to verify: that Thomas had a spiritual purpose, but an important element of that purpose was its concealment. We know that to most of his contemporaries, including the monks of Christ Church, it remained successfully concealed throughout his life.

But there is another aspect of Thomas's 'conversion' that continues to raise questions. That is, that whatever change Thomas underwent on becoming archbishop, it was not a definitive break with what had gone before, nor did it open a direct path to sanctity. Thomas's life before his consecration, if worldly and undistinguished by obvious sanctity, was not that of an irreligious sinner. To his enemies, he remained the proud chancellor in a different and more dangerous guise, and Thomas himself later confessed that he did not always live up to the office of archbishop. As one modern historian has written, his was 'not in the deepest sense a conversion', nor 'a transformation or rebirth of character'. He did not 'pass at a definite moment with Paul, with Augustine, with Francis, into a new world of the spirit from the world of other men'.[9] But the fact is that despite the biblical language, Thomas's biographers do not claim that he experienced a conversion along the lines of St Paul. For them the change was indeed great and dramatic, but it was also just one especially significant step on his path to perfection. In fact, the language used of Thomas's transformation was that commonly used in twelfth-century England to describe those who entered upon a new vocation – those who adopted the monastic life or joined a new religious order, or even those who took on a new responsibility, such as a bishop, archbishop or abbot.[10]

It makes sense, then, that looking back on Thomas's early days as archbishop from the vantage point of his death, those monastic writers such as William of Canterbury should describe it in terms of the new life of a monk, emphasizing his prayers and mortifications. But even the monks of Canterbury would have recognized that it was not enough for a successful archbishop to be pious. The archbishop had a range of duties which placed great demands on him, and it was customary for twelfth-century prelates to bemoan the pressure of business and the lack of leisure for the things of God. He had specific liturgical duties: to confirm the faithful, to ordain priests and to consecrate churches within his archdiocese. He was a major landlord, with responsibility to protect the lands he had inherited against incursion, and to extend the wealth of his see where possible. This meant that he was a feudal overlord, with many tenants, and many obligations to them. He oversaw an extensive administrative machine, geared towards the running of the secular and spiritual obligations of office. He was a judge, presiding in court over disputes within the archdiocese, and the leader of the English Church, holding synodal gatherings of prelates and abbot. He was also one of the principal vassals of the king – a 'tenant-in-chief' – owing the provision of troops to the king and attendance at his court. Inevitably, the archbishop of Canterbury was consulted on matters of state and acted as a conduit between the demands of the English hierarchy, the king and the pope. Not surprisingly, some archbishops were not up to the task.

Some, such as the rapaciously ambitious Stigand in the eleventh century, found themselves so engaged in worldly business that the position of archbishop became a travesty. Anselm, who held the office at the turn of the twelfth century, was one of the most gifted and saintly archbishops of Canterbury but was considered a failure by many on account of his aversion to worldly affairs.

To his biographers, Thomas succeeded in perfectly balancing the dual nature of the position. Citing the standard biblical examples of the contemplative and active lives, they say he was like Mary of Bethany who sat at the feet of Jesus, feasting on the bread of angels, he who had previously starved now being filled; but he did not neglect the work of Mary's sister Martha, busy about many things.[11] John of Salisbury tells us that whatever time Thomas could withdraw from pressing business he almost always gave to prayer and reading. At the same time, the reverence he showed in celebrating Mass also informed the faith and morals of those around him, and in his preaching he acted as teacher and pastor. Even in precious clothes he was a pauper in spirit, with a happy face he maintained a contrite heart. He was mild and gentle to the meek and the poor, but freely condemned the vices of the powerful.[12]

The daily life of a twelfth-century churchman was strictly laid out, and although there were variations throughout the year, and an inevitable distance between theory and practice, there was an expectation that it conform to an established programme. The monks of Canterbury followed a daily round based on the sixth-century Rule of St Benedict. The day was marked by communal prayers – the offices of Matins, Lauds, Prime, Terce, Sext, Nones, Vespers and Compline – in addition to two Masses a day, private periods of prayer and reading and some work. It was impossible for an archbishop to conform fully to this model – his calling was not exclusively one of prayer, and there were many demands upon him – but he would have followed a modified version of the monastic *horarium* or 'hours'.

Herbert of Bosham gives a detailed account of Thomas's daily life in the early days of his archiepiscopate, explaining that 'nobody's life is truly portrayed if where and how he lived is omitted.'[13] In his account, Thomas rose immediately after cockcrow and chanted the office. Then thirteen poor men were shown into a private chamber where the archbishop would wash their feet and give them each four silver coins. After a brief nap, Thomas would turn to reading the Scriptures, 'so that by a new learning his former ignorance which for so long a time he had contracted from the world would be overcome, and a new image of the archbishop would be formed in the pontiff'.[14] Herbert himself was the archbishop's teacher in Bible studies and with his help Thomas soon became learned and developed a great enthusiasm for the Bible. He would even carry pages of scripture rolled up in his sleeves wherever he went so that he would always have some edifying reading available. About nine he left his chamber and went to say Mass, though, as Herbert notes, he did not say Mass every day. He also tells us that Thomas was prone to vain and wandering thoughts during Mass, so he tended to hurry through the readings. Next the archbishop left the church and entered the court room. Church courts were very active, dealing with cases of land tenure, felonies, presentation to churches and appeals from lower courts, all of which Thomas would have had to judge. He was, says Herbert, 'as great a judge at the tribunal as he was as a priest at the altar',[15] and notable for not accepting gifts.

A little after noon, the archbishop dined. 'The life of anyone is not described', writes Herbert, 'if his nourishment for this life, without which this present life cannot go on, is overlooked.'[16] He goes into lavish detail about Thomas's table. Thomas sat in the middle of the table, with his learned companions on the right, and the monks and other religious on the left, household clerks also seated nearby, and visiting laymen at a separate table. They were served by a swarm of attendants, noble youths, 'like purple and rose-coloured spring flowers',[17] whom their fathers had committed to the archbishop's court, the most noble being the king's eldest son, Henry. Although Thomas remained temperate amid such splendour, secretly sharing some of his food with other guests, Herbert acknowledges that this magnificent table appears more like that of an emperor than an archbishop, and very different to the simple fare of Christ's apostles. But we should remember, says Herbert, that St Paul made himself 'all things to all men', and that the Scriptures say that 'All things have their seasons, a time to weep and a time to laugh; a time to mourn and a time to dance.'[18] Thomas's day showed him in a variety of guises, 'now in a hairshirt ministering to the poor at table; now in a stole serving the faithful at the altar; now in a breastplate of justice putting an end to lawsuits at court; now with temperance rejoicing with the other diners at the banquet'.[19] And this is the image of Thomas as archbishop that Herbert upholds: a man performing many roles, and each of them admirably.

The Break with the King

The question of Thomas's 'conversion' is of course closely bound up with that of his conflict with the king. Was the dispute a consequence of Thomas's new spiritual purpose and dedication to the Church, or did the rift with the king open up for Thomas a new awareness of his duties as archbishop and deepen his religious instincts? Surely both are true. Thomas does seem to have approached his obligations as archbishop with a new zeal, which took the king by surprise. At the same time, the archbishop's conflicts and trials are presented as strengthening his spiritual purpose. If we believe Thomas's supporters, the inward transformation and the outward embrace of ecclesiastical rights acted upon each other and were mutually reinforcing, all the way up to his last moments.

But we must also acknowledge that 'the Becket dispute' did not begin and end with Thomas Becket himself. Thomas entered the archiepiscopate at a time when England was facing countervailing pressures as regards the relationship between the Church and the crown. Henry II was determined to take action to settle some of these matters, notably in relation to spheres of jurisdiction, just as upon his accession he took concerted action to reconfigure the relationship between the crown and the nobility. The evidence would suggest that Henry had installed Thomas as archbishop with the expectation that he would facilitate this programme. We can call it, as the king's supporters did, an attempt to restore the established rights of the kings of England, or we can call it, as did Thomas's supporters, a tyrannical usurpation of the Church's rights. What is clear is that Henry was intent on introducing reform to the relationship between crown and Church, one that was conservative in its objectives but often radical in its methods, just as his earlier reforms had been. What this meant was that the leaders of the English Church needed to respond, and the way they responded determined the nature of the dispute. Henry's attempts to clarify the relationship between royal and ecclesiastical power would have created tension and division no matter who was archbishop. But no one could have guessed how explosive the fallout would be under Thomas Becket.

Even with all the commentary about Thomas's change of heart upon becoming archbishop, no major issues came between him and King Henry in his first year in office. This is despite the fact that Thomas gave a clear signal of independence soon after his appointment by resigning as chancellor. Henry had intended that Thomas would continue in this office when he became archbishop. Such an arrangement existed in Germany, where Rainald of Dassel continued as chancellor and leading advisor to Emperor Frederick 'Barbarossa' when he was appointed archbishop of Cologne in 1159, and after Henry II's death it would become normal in England too for bishops and archbishops to hold such major offices of state as chancellor or justiciar. But Thomas reportedly sent a messenger to the king informing him that he was giving up the chancellorship on account of the burden of his work, to which the king responded, 'He doesn't care about serving me – that's very clear!'[20] Another of Thomas's early moves was to demand back certain lands that he claimed had been taken away from the church of Canterbury during the time of his predecessors. Disputes over land were commonplace in twelfth-century England, and it was the duty of any archbishop to protect the rights of the Church that had been committed to him. Nonetheless the assertive reclamation of estates had the potential to provoke the king, especially when, as in this case, many of the disputed lands were held by Henry's most powerful tenants. Even so, it is said that these magnates were slow to complain to the king because they knew how well disposed Henry was to his new archbishop.[21]

The chances of conflict were also minimized by the fact that King Henry was away from England in his continental lands until January 1163. Thomas raced to meet him on his return at the port of Southampton where, according to Herbert of Bosham, they showered embraces and kisses on each other, each trying to outdo the other in bestowing honour.[22] In his first year in office Thomas also had the opportunity to attend a papal council. The Italian lawyer Roland Bandinelli had been appointed Pope Alexander III in 1159, but the election was disputed by a faction backed by Emperor Frederick, who set up a rival or 'antipope' as Victor IV. So began a long drawn-out schism within the Church, which led Alexander to flee Italy for France. With royal approval, Thomas sailed to Flanders and made his way through Normandy and Maine to the city of Tours, where the pope had convened a gathering of the cardinals and leading ecclesiastics of the western Church in May 1163. Herbert, who accompanied Thomas, says that the archbishop's reputation was so great that as he was approaching the city, the citizens and locals, the visiting archbishops and bishops, and almost all the cardinals came out to meet him. When he came to give his respects to the pope, it was Alexander who rose to greet Thomas and give him reverence. When the business of the Council of Tours was completed, Thomas returned in joy and prosperity to England, where he was received by the king 'as if a father by his son'. But, adds Herbert, nothing in life lasts forever or stays the same, there is 'a time to weep and a time to laugh, a time to love and a time to hate, a time for war and a time for peace: for everything there is a season'. It would have been difficult to find anywhere else in the world such a great king and so great an archbishop, and such harmony between such great men. But if the harmony was great, its duration was brief.[23]

Even if Herbert is here exaggerating the mutual love of archbishop and king so as to make the breach between them all the more dramatic, the evidence broadly suggests that 'the Becket dispute' was one that emerged slowly and gathered momentum until the former friends had become irreconcilable. As Thomas began his second year as archbishop, more direct differences emerged. In July 1163 the king summoned the bishops and nobles of the realm to his lodge at Woodstock, where he proposed a new arrangement for the support of his sheriffs. Traditionally, the bishops and nobles had made a direct payment annually to these local officials for their well-being, but the king now attempted to redirect that fee to the royal exchequer. Thomas rejected this demand, insisting that this 'sheriff's aid' was a voluntary payment

and should not be changed to a legally enforceable royal exac-
tion, and the king backed down.[24] Soon after, the king complained
about the archbishop's excommunication of a baron named
William of Eynsford, who had allegedly mistreated some clerks.[25]
Excommunication placed the transgressor outside of the community of the faithful. It was one of the Church's most powerful
disciplinary sanctions, and in a society that depended upon
personal charisma, loyalty and connections, it was one to be
dreaded.[26] But the king argued that William ought not to have
been excommunicated without his consent, because he was
one of the king's senior vassals (or 'tenants-in-chief'), and here
Thomas backed down and absolved him.

   These disputes were just the prelude to a more contentious
case that focused attention on a fundamental point of tension
between the crown and the Church. This was the case of Philip
de Broi, a canon of Bedford who had been accused of killing a
certain knight. Twelfth-century England was a land in which
many courts existed, each with its own jurisdiction. Henry II's
reign is known as the crucial period in the development of the
English common law, when royal justice gained a wider reach
as it became more systematic and easier to access. But this was
not the only legal system that existed. As we have seen, Thomas
the chancellor served as a royal justice, but he also acted as a
judge in his own court when he became archbishop. Since the
time of the Conqueror, ecclesiastical courts had judged on matters of morals and faith, on disputes concerning such matters as
Church property, and on cases of misconduct involving those in
religious orders. Other kinds of cases could be tried in civil courts,
including the manor court, the county court and the hundred
court. Because Philip was a canon – a man living in religious
orders – he was tried by a Church court, and in this case he
attested to his innocence under oath, and was set free. A local
royal justice then tried to reopen the case, but Philip refused to

answer for a charge on which he had already been judged, and threw insults at the royal justice, who now complained to the king. The king directed Archbishop Thomas to take up the case in his court at Canterbury. There it was judged that Philip could not be tried again for homicide, but for his insult to the king's justice he was sentenced to a fine, a scourging and exile. To the king, this fell well short of a suitable penalty.[27]

Henry II had become increasingly concerned about the problem of how to punish churchmen who had been found guilty of a serious felony. By the 1160s the numbers in religious orders had grown, and crime among this group had become a more pressing issue. Those in religious orders included not only priests, monks, bishops and abbots, but clerks. To the king, the failure of ecclesiastical courts to punish 'criminous clerks', as modern historians have called them, threatened peace and order in the kingdom. Not only that, the undue leniency afforded to these men by ecclesiastical courts served to undermine the king's authority.[28]

Prompted by the case of Philip de Broi, and other similar cases, Henry summoned all the senior ecclesiastics to a council at Westminster in October 1163.[29] There he complained of the disturbance of the peace of the kingdom, and proposed that clerks convicted in an ecclesiastical court of a serious crime be transferred immediately to royal magistrates, who would strip them of their ecclesiastical protection and inflict physical punishment upon them. Royal officials would be present when clerks were stripped of their ecclesiastical orders, so they might be seized immediately and not flee. Thomas's biographers present some of the arguments made by the king, or by sympathetic bishops, to Thomas. One was that canon law in some circumstances sanctioned the handing over of the clergy to secular courts upon their deposition. Another was an appeal to the Old Testament, where the priests and Levites were not exempted from the Law of Moses but rather were judged more severely because they held a greater dignity in society. On the other side it is reported that Thomas cited a long list of canons that prohibited the handing over of clergy to secular judgement. He also cited the biblical reading 'God does not judge twice for the same thing,'[30] arguing that this meant that a clerk should not face a punishment in a secular court when he had already been punished in an ecclesiastical court by being stripped of his office. When the bishops withdrew to confer on this, some reportedly favoured acquiescing to the king's demands, but they returned to the king with a unanimous rejection of his proposal.

Now the king tried a different approach, one that would have far-reaching consequences. Instead of focusing on the specific issue of 'criminous clerks', he made a broader demand that the prelates 'obey his royal customs in every respect'. What Henry meant was that he should enjoy the same rights that his royal ancestors had been able to enjoy. This demand was quite consistent with his ambition to restore royal authority that had been evident since his accession in 1154, but for the leaders of the Church, such an acknowledgement would have given innumerable hostages to fortune. Who was to determine what were the royal customs that Henry's predecessors enjoyed? What would happen when a royal custom conflicted with rights that the Church claimed? Would ecclesiastics find themselves bound to forfeit their historical privileges in favour of the king's demands? It was not altogether surprising, then, that Thomas responded to the king's demands by declaring that the bishops would obey the royal customs in every way but with the qualification, 'saving our order'. In other words, they would obey the royal customs where they did not conflict with their own rights. When Henry demanded the same of the other bishops, they all echoed Thomas's answer (apart from Bishop Hilary of Chichester, who chose his own qualifying formula). The king in fury departed from the bishops without saying farewell. The next day, he made his displeasure felt by ordering the archbishop to surrender all the castles and estates he had entrusted to his custody, and by removing his young son Henry from Thomas's household.

Regnum and Sacerdotium

The Council of Westminster had begun on Sunday, 13 October, with an important and elaborate ceremony in Westminster Abbey. On that day the body of King Edward the Confessor was raised to a splendid new tomb above ground, in the presence of the monks of Westminster, the king, nobles and prelates.[31] King Edward's death in 1066 had ushered in the succession crisis that culminated in the Conquest of England, and since then he had developed a reputation for sanctity, forcefully promoted by King Henry II, who was related to him through his mother Matilda. Pope Alexander had approved King Edward's canonization in February 1161, and this ceremony of 'translation' to a new tomb was a further public step in promoting the cult of St Edward. It was also a statement by the king about an ideal of Christian kingship. Henry II is considered to have been a man of personal piety, and he could look back to a long line of English kings who had been recognized as saints, including the seventh-century king of Northumbria, Oswald, and the tenth-century King Edward the Martyr. There were many examples of other kings who stood as models of cooperation with the Church. King Edgar had worked with Archbishop Dunstan in Canterbury in reforming the English Church in the tenth century after the ravages of the Vikings, and even such an acquisitive king as William the Conqueror had deferred in many respects to his archbishop, Lanfranc. Kings and churchmen alike had older examples of virtuous rulers: the biblical King David who confessed his sins and honoured God, Emperor Constantine I who converted to Christianity and was praised as a supporter of the

English school, *Edward the Confessor*, c. 1450, oil and tempera on oak panel (from a rood screen).

Church, his successor Emperor Theodosius, who bowed to the correction of the Church.

There were also examples of tyrants who ruled in their own interests, not God's: Herod, who sought to kill Jesus; the Roman emperors Nero and Diocletian who persecuted the early Christians; and a host of other secular rulers who did not observe their duties to the Church and its representatives. England too had kings who were condemned for their immorality and hostility to the Church – for example the Conqueror's son, William 'Rufus', whose unexpected death, pierced by an arrow while out hunting, was widely interpreted as divine punishment. Most kings were neither saints nor tyrants, though, and instead sought to promote a good relationship with the Church that did not damage their own interests. They acknowledged that they held their offices by the grace of God, that they depended on the ideological legitimation of their position by the priesthood, and the prayers of the faithful for their salvation. Churchmen needed the physical protection of the secular power, and they relied on kings and princes to provide for church buildings and personnel, and to establish an order within their lands in which religion could flourish. But they also recognized that a good relationship could be difficult to achieve. Thomas's predecessor, Archbishop Anselm, described the English Church as a plough drawn by two oxen – the king and the archbishop of Canterbury – one ruling 'by human justice and sovereignty, the other by divine doctrine and authority'.[32] The plough is the contract between the kingship (*regnum*) and the priesthood (*sacerdotium*), and those who pull the plough are the individual kings and archbishops who determine how this contract is fulfilled.

The century before the Becket conflict had seen momentous changes in the relationship between royal and priestly power. In the mid-eleventh century a reform movement emerged within the Church, initially focused on moral renewal and the elimination of such abuses as clerical marriage and the selling of Church offices. The pontificate of Gregory VII (1073–85), however, witnessed a direct confrontation between the papacy and the German emperor over the issue of 'lay investiture' – the granting by laymen of the symbols of office to senior ecclesiastics. This led to Pope Gregory's excommunication and deposition of Emperor Henry IV, and eventually civil war. Though the dispute ended in compromise, its most significant outcome was the enhanced status of the papacy. Gregory's vision was of a papal power that crossed national boundaries and governed the lives of not only the clergy but all Christians. It gained expression in papal leadership of the Crusades, which began in the 1090s, and in the development of mechanisms of papal government: the college of cardinals, papal legates and the systematization of canon law.

Many of those who held high positions in the English Church in the 1160s had studied in the continental schools where 'High Church' theories about the superiority of the spiritual sphere over the temporal were disseminated.[33] Herbert of Bosham studied and taught such theories in Paris before joining Thomas's service, and he attributes to Thomas a speech at the Council of Westminster that directly reflects such ideas. He has Thomas argue before the king that the clergy, being set apart from the rest of society and given over to the Lord's work, are not subject to but superior to earthly kings. They appoint kings, and it is from them that the king receives his powers. Therefore, not only do kings have no jurisdiction in matters of the Church, but the clergy are the judges of kings, as it says in the Bible, 'They bind their kings with chains and their nobles with fetters of iron.'[34] Significantly, such theories were known and widely accepted well beyond Thomas's inner circle. If pressed, all of the English episcopate would have accepted the superiority of the spiritual power over the temporal, and upheld the principle of ecclesiastical liberty. But – and this is a crucial point – that did not mean that they considered that such principles merited conflict with the king. We will see again and again Thomas's episcopal colleagues clashing with him, not on principle but on tactics.[35]

King Henry, too, could see that episcopal support was Thomas's weak point. The other bishops may support Thomas on principle, but not necessarily his approach to remedying the problem. Over the weeks and months following the Council of Westminster, Henry put pressure on Thomas and strove to isolate him from his peers. He summoned those whom he considered the most pliable – Roger, archbishop of York, Gilbert, bishop of London, and Hilary, bishop of Chichester – all of whom agreed to submit to the customs once he had assured them that he would demand nothing that would go against clerical rights. Next those whom the king had turned began to work on the archbishop. Hilary of Chichester visited Thomas and tried to assure him that the Church had nothing to fear from acquiescence in the king's customs. 'What', asked Hilary, 'is this evil that is so great and appalling that you alone see and understand it and no one else?' Then Abbot Philip of Aumône, sent by the pope to restore peace, presented Thomas with letters from the papal curia reminding him that the Church was at that moment divided by schism and depended on the support of the king of England. Thomas was warned that such dangerous times called for expediency, that this was not a time for a ruler of the Church to exercise severity, but rather for dissimulation and toleration.[36] Swayed by such advice, Thomas went to see the king at Woodstock around Christmas. There he told the king that not wishing to impose any obstacle to his goodwill, he was prepared to observe the customs of the realm in good faith. Henry answered that since Thomas had shown himself so defiant in public on this matter, and offended his honour in such a way, he must now have his concession to his customs similarly acknowledged in public before all the bishops, abbots and nobles of the realm.[37]

Clarendon, January 1164

The venue chosen for this public concession to the king's customs was his hunting lodge at Clarendon, in late January 1164. To this gathering Henry called all of the most important individuals in the land. This was well before parliament had developed in England as a way of regularly meeting to discuss great matters of state but already it was common for the king to consult with the most powerful figures in the land when an important enough issue arose. That Henry saw Thomas's acceptance of the royal customs as one such occasion is clear from the distinguished group that gathered at Clarendon. They included England's two archbishops, and all but three of the bishops. Henry's son and heir, Henry, was there, as were ten earls, numerous barons and all the senior figures in the royal administration.[38]

King Henry opened by declaring that since various disputes had arisen about the rights of the crown on the one hand, and the rights of the Church on the other, he wanted all the bishops to give their express, absolute and unconditional consent to the customs and privileges that had been observed in the time of his grandfather King Henry I. The response of the bishops, not just Thomas but many others, was to resist this demand. Thomas's biographers say that the archbishop could immediately see that to do otherwise would put the Church in danger, and he preferred to incur the king's anger than to abandon God's law. He certainly incurred the anger of the king, who issued furious threats against the ecclesiastics, while his attendants ran this way and that, their aggressive demeanour filling everyone with dread. The bishops were then shut up in a room apart from the laymen for two full days to deliberate, and eventually some of their number began to detach themselves from the wall of consensus. Jocelin of Salisbury and William of Norwich, both of whom were already out of favour with the king, begged the archbishop to have pity on them, fearing that they would be singled out for severe reprisals. Next the earls of Leicester and Cornwall warned Thomas that unless he speedily satisfied the king, they would be obliged to carry out the king's revenge upon the bishops. Then the master of the Templars in England – the military order of Jerusalem established after the First Crusade – and one of his colleagues spoke to Thomas. They assured him that all he had to do was to satisfy the king verbally, and he would never hear mention of the customs again, and full peace would be restored between them. Moved by their pleas, Thomas said that having received reassurances, he was prepared to keep the customs of the realm 'in the word of truth'.

As soon as Thomas gave this commitment, the king demanded that the other bishops do the same, and they did. But then the king took matters one step further. In order to avoid any contradiction in the future, he said, the senior nobles would now go out with his clerks to recollect the customs of his grandfather and have them written down.[39] In other words, whereas the bishops believed they were giving their verbal consent to the king's vaguely expressed 'customs', they were now about to be presented with an itemized list of what he claimed were the rights of the king of England in respect to the Church, put down in writing for all posterity. According to the king's command the customs were then written down, along with a statement of acknowledgement by the bishops and a list of witnesses, in the form of a *chirograph* – a type of memorandum in which each party takes a copy. One copy was given to Archbishop Roger of York, another to Thomas, and the third kept by the king. Now the king made a further demand: that the archbishop affix his seal to the chirograph, thereby confirming his assent. To which Thomas reportedly replied, 'By Almighty God, never while I am living will my seal be put to these.'[40]

These 'royal customs' have gone down in history as The Constitutions of Clarendon.[41] Although other issues came to complicate the conflict between Henry and Thomas, these were seen at the time, and have been ever since, as central to the dispute. Herbert of Bosham went so far as to call them 'the full cause of dissension . . . the reason for exile and martyrdom'.[42] The Constitutions comprise sixteen clauses, which are claimed to represent 'royal customs and privileges'. Not all were contentious, but most were seen as clear violations of ecclesiastical liberty. Five clauses concern matters of ecclesiastical jurisdiction, and the most controversial of these addresses the issue of criminous clerks:

> Clerks charged and accused of any offence, when
> summoned by the king's justice, shall come to his court
> to answer there concerning what seems to the king's court
> ought to be answered there, and in the ecclesiastical court
> for what seems ought to be answered there, but in such a
> way that the justice of the king sends men into the court
> of Holy Church to see in what way it is tried there. And
> if the clerk should be convicted or confesses, the Church
> ought no longer protect him.[43]

The precise meaning of this clause has been much debated, but what appears to be asserted is that anyone accused of a criminal offence should first come before the king's court. If the accused is an ecclesiastic, the case may then be referred to the ecclesiastical court, but he will be accompanied there by a royal officer. If the accused is then convicted in the ecclesiastical court, he will be stripped of his protection as a churchman and handed over for punishment to the royal court. This, of course, directly addressed the issue raised by the case of Philip de Broi and other 'criminous clerks' and resolved it in a way that acknowledged the role of Church courts but also allowed for the authority of royal justice in punishing criminals, whether laymen or clergy.

We have already seen how Thomas's use of the power of excommunication brought him into dispute with the king, and this issue is also addressed in the Constitutions where it is stated that no tenant-in-chief of the king or any of the ministers of his demesne (that is, the land directly under royal control) should be excommunicated, or their lands placed under interdict, without approaching the king first, or his justiciar if the king is out of the country.[44] Another clause addresses the issue of vacancies, stating that when an archbishopric or a bishopric, or an abbey or priory in the royal demesne, is vacant, it ought to remain in the king's hands and he ought to receive all revenues and duties until it is filled. One issue that as yet had made little impact on Thomas's archiepiscopate but would soon prove of major consequence was that of relations with the pope. The Constitutions prohibited senior clergy from leaving the realm without the king's licence.[45] The attempt to regulate travel outside the realm by ecclesiastics was but one reflection of the growing influence of the papacy in twelfth-century England. This was evident in papal representatives visiting England more frequently, and a concomitant increase in traffic of ecclesiastics from England to Rome. In recent years too, churchmen in England had begun to appeal in growing numbers to papal jurisdiction, a matter that the Constitutions addressed by prohibiting appeals by churchmen to the pope without the king's licence.[46] As it turned out, the Becket dispute would do much to encourage the practice of such appeals, as both Thomas and his critics resorted repeatedly to the papal curia as a means of limiting their opponents' scope for action.

When Thomas – and many other leaders of the English Church – referred to the Constitutions, however, they tended to approach them as a whole rather than in their individual clauses. The multifaceted danger they posed is expressed well by William fitz Stephen, who lists some of the Constitutions in his Life of St Thomas and comments:

But these constitutions had never been written down
before, nor indeed had existed before in the kingdom
of England. And even if they had been, though the
king upheld these spurious statutes on the basis of
antiquity and custom rather than on right, he should
have remembered that the Lord said, 'Keep my laws',
and, 'Alas for those who condone unjust laws'. And
while the Lord did say, 'I am truth', he is never found
to have said, 'I am custom'.[47]

The first point is perhaps the most perceptive: that the central
problem with the Constitutions was the fact that they were written down. This is something that another shrewd observer noted
too. Two years later, in 1166, Herbert of Bosham had an interview
with King Henry in which, reviewing the dispute, he expressed his
amazement that the king should have put his customs in writing.
For, he explained, evil customs contrary to the Church may also
be found in other lands, but they are not written down, and therefore there is a better chance that they may be annulled.[48] In this
regard the Constitutions can be seen as one landmark in a broader
movement towards the formulation of relationships, and their
expression in writing. They stand between two more famous examples. In 1086 King William I's commissioners toured England
examining lands and possessions, and what was owed to the
crown, and these records were written down in the Domesday
Book, called that because its sentences were as definite and un-
alterable as Judgement Day. Later, in 1215, the barons of England
constrained King John to accept certain restraints on his power
and to guarantee certain rights of the Church and nobility and
gave them formal written expression in the document known as
Magna Carta. The Constitutions of Clarendon were perhaps
more modest in their ambition, but they can nonetheless be seen
in hindsight as part of the same trend towards written codification

of what were previously unwritten customs.[49] Fitz Stephen's second argument is that what Henry II claimed to be ancestral customs were nothing of the sort. In other words, rather than reflecting the reality in the time of Henry I and his predecessors, these were innovations. The extent to which the 'customs' represented earlier practice has long exercised legal historians. But the most common line of argument against the Constitutions went beyond the specific details of whether a custom had existed in the past. Rather, it was that even if such customs had existed before, they ought not to be sustained in the future, for God's law is superior to the king's customs. Such considerations would move the dispute on to deeper questions of truth, justice, the king's honour and God's honour.

A Moment of Clarification

At Clarendon Henry and Thomas had stated more clearly than ever before what they wanted for the crown and the Church respectively. The king had presented what he claimed were the ancestral rights of the crown as regards the Church, and asked that they be acknowledged publicly. The archbishop had sought that any recognition of royal privileges should not infringe upon the liberty of the Church. Neither achieved what they wanted, but the outcome was worse for each of them than simply a failure to achieve their objectives. Both Henry and Thomas left Clarendon with damage done to their own reputations, and resentment built up against them for the future. Their actions in January 1164 would be recalled by their enemies for many years after, and even as other disputes emerged between king and archbishop during those years, the Constitutions would never be removed as a bone of contention.

Had Thomas and his fellow prelates given their full consent to them, the Constitutions might have been regarded by history as another important piece of Henry's reforming strategy. But they were never likely to gain easy acceptance, and Henry seems to have overstepped in turning a general recognition of his rights into a detailed statement of what those rights were. He raised the stakes by putting them in writing, and by attempting to pressure Thomas to accept the written customs without a chance to consult his brethren. According to one account, when Thomas left Clarendon he was consoled by one thing: that previously the traps he and the Church had faced had been hidden, but now they were out in the open. Another says that Thomas took his part of the chirograph with him so that he could have before him a reminder and a warning of the king's deviousness and evil intent. In other words, at Clarendon the king put his cards on the table, and Thomas took a lasting lesson from it. Over the following years no assurances of the king's good faith would succeed in bringing Thomas to compromise.

But if Clarendon was a setback for Henry, it was a disaster for Thomas. Inevitably, it chilled his relationship with the king even further. Soon after, according to one account, Thomas attempted to visit the king in his hunting lodge at Woodstock but had the gates shut in his face. Others say that the archbishop tried to flee the realm but was turned back by contrary winds, which Thomas interpreted as God's judgement that he must face further trials. But worse was that at Clarendon, unlike earlier at Westminster, Thomas alienated not only the king but many within the Church. A few years later, Bishop Gilbert of London wrote a scathing letter to Thomas in which he recalled how at Clarendon all the other senior clergy had stood firm and unafraid, willing to suffer to the death in defence of the Church's liberty. 'Who fled? Who turned tail? Who was broken in spirit?', demanded Gilbert. 'The leader of the army turned tail, the commander of the battlefield ran away, the archbishop of Canterbury departed from the common counsel and association of his brothers.'[50] If Thomas's sin

in the king's eyes was in failing to put his seal to their agreement, his sin in the eyes of many within the Church was that
he accepted the customs in the first place. Another account tells
that after Clarendon Thomas was rebuked by his cross-bearer,
Alexander Llewelyn, who demanded of him, 'What virtue is left
to him who has betrayed his conscience and reputation?'[51]

Herbert of Bosham tells a story of Thomas's remorse, and
here, as in his account of Thomas's reflections on election as
archbishop, the scene is the road to Canterbury. On the journey
back from Clarendon, the archbishop seemed unusually dis-
quieted and Herbert asked him the reason. Thomas replied, 'No
wonder I now seem like that when the English Church which
my predecessors, as the world knows, ruled so prudently amongst
so many dangers, should through my sins be delivered into slav-
ery.' Those earlier archbishops had fought bravely for the Church,
he says, but under his rule the Church has suffered, and the reason
is clear: because he was raised to this office not from the Church
but from the court.

> Not from the cloister, not from any place of religion,
> not from the company of the Saviour, but rather from
> the retinue of Caesar, proud and vain, from a keeper of
> hawks I was made shepherd of the sheep. From a patron
> of actors and a follower of hounds, I was made pastor of
> so many souls.

To this confession Herbert responded with encouraging words.
'If you fell disgracefully,' he told the archbishop, 'revive more
strongly and more decently, and examine yourself.' He reminded
him of the examples of St Peter who denied Christ but became
the leader of the Church, of King David who was once a traitor
and adulterer, but became the model king of Israel, and St Paul,
who was once Saul, an apostate of the Church. 'You were at one

time, as it seemed then, and was said thus, Saul,' said Herbert.
'But now if you wish to be Paul, having removed the scales from
your eyes, Jesus will show you by his work how much you ought
to suffer for His sake.'[52]

Sts Stephen, Thomas Becket and Nicholas of Bari, 13th century,
fresco, Sanctuary of the Sacro Speco, Subiaco.

FOUR

Trial and Exile

Well before the murder in the cathedral, observers of the dispute between Thomas and Henry realized that they were witnessing historic events, and began to record them as they happened. The years from 1164 to 1166 were among the most eventful in Thomas's life, and we can follow many of the public dramas in which he was involved in close detail thanks to the contemporary accounts written by his friends and critics. The year 1164 began with Henry II seeking to turn Thomas to his will at the Council of Clarendon, but it ended with the king and archbishop farther away than ever. Henry summoned Thomas to trial at Northampton in October 1164 in the hope of humbling the archbishop or removing him from office, and Thomas responded with a defiance that his supporters saw as a foreshadowing of his martyrdom. He then fled into exile in France where he made his case before the pope, and was sent to live in a remote monastery in Burgundy. But although Thomas retreated for a time to a life of prayer and asceticism, by 1166 he was ready to rouse himself to action against what he considered to be the enemies of the Church.

One of the lessons of this period is that there was nothing inevitable about how the Becket dispute played out. Contemporaries suggested that the king's determination to exploit his privileges in relation to the Church, or alternatively the archbishop's unsuitability for office, ensured an inexorable collision between them. Modern historians have suggested that the dispute brought to the surface uncontainable tensions between Church and crown. But it is also clear that from the moment that Henry II first raised the issue of his ancestral customs he and Thomas faced a range of choices. And from 1164 onwards both king and archbishop tended to choose the most polarizing options open to them, as each sought victory rather than compromise. This caused participants and onlookers to view the dispute in a different way. While the issues at stake often concerned mundane business – financial, legal and political – they were increasingly couched in transcendent terms of right and wrong, good and evil. Biblical language of trial and suffering, righteousness and tyranny came to be applied by contemporaries to the events of their day, for already they were being seen as part of a momentous and memorable struggle.

Northampton, October 1164

After Clarendon, Thomas continued to fulfil his duties as archbishop, and he even appeared with the king at the consecration of Reading Abbey on 19 April, where Henry's grandfather King Henry I lay buried.[1] But otherwise the normal relationship between a king and archbishop was all but suspended. Neither seems to have been under any illusion as to a speedy improvement in relations. Early in the year, Thomas sent his clerk John of Salisbury to Paris to gather support, and perhaps to prepare the way for exile. Henry seems to have been searching for an opportunity to remove Thomas from office, and one presented itself in the summer of 1164. As was the case with the Constitutions of Clarendon, it began with a relatively trivial issue. John fitz Gilbert, Marshal of the Exchequer, claimed that a certain parcel of land in one of the archbishop's estates belonged to him by right, but when he took his case to the

archbishop's court he gained no satisfaction. John then secured
a royal writ summoning Thomas to appear before the king's
court to answer the charge that he had failed to do justice to
John in his court. On the day assigned, 14 September, Thomas
did not turn up and instead sent some of his men to rebut the
charges. This allowed the king to call the archbishop to trial on
the secular charge of failing to do justice to John, and also for
contempt to the king's majesty. He was summoned to Northampton
on 6 October to answer before the king and the bishops, abbots,
earls and barons of the land.[2]

The Council of Northampton was a trial in the sense of a
judicial procedure before the king, the bishops, abbots, earls
and barons of the land. It was also a trial of strength in which
Henry II pressed Thomas in every way he could to submit entirely
to his will or else resign his office. But to Thomas and his supporters it also recalled another kind of trial, the kind endured
by Christ, the apostles and the early martyrs. In such trials victory
was achieved by endurance and suffering, and the more the secular powers assailed the victim the more the victim triumphed.
Those persecuted by earthly forces had their own spiritual weapons, and what looked like defeat and humiliation to the world
could in truth mean a greater victory. It is to this idea of a trial
that Thomas finally resorted, finding victory in adversity, or as
William fitz Stephen, our best witness to these events, puts it,
'a martyrdom in the spirit'.[3]

That this was to be no ordinary trial was soon made clear by
various signs. Instead of the customary summons from the king
it was left to the sheriff of Kent to summon the archbishop to
Northampton. When he arrived at the town, Thomas found that
his lodgings had been occupied by soldiers of one of the king's
men, with the king's knowledge. Henry himself was still hawking along the nearby rivers and streams, and so kept Thomas
waiting until the next day to begin proceedings. The next

morning Thomas came to greet the king outside his chapel, but the king did not offer him the kiss of peace. And since John the Marshal was occupied on the king's business at the exchequer in London, the trial was put off for another day. All of these were public indications of the king's hostility, intended to signal not only to Thomas but to the lay magnates and the senior ecclesiastics assembled that the archbishop had lost the king's favour, and that there was no benefit in taking his side.

The trial proper began on Thursday, 8 October, in the royal castle of Northampton.[4] The king and archbishop did not face each other directly. Henry and his clerks took their places in an upper room, Thomas and his men sat in a lower hall, and the other magnates moved between the two. The case for which Thomas had been called was disposed of quickly. Thomas was accused of contempt of the crown because he had failed to come in person to answer the king's summons in the case of John the Marshal, nor had he made an adequate excuse. The archbishop attempted to rebut the charges but he was not heeded, and the king demanded that he be condemned to forfeit all his movable goods at the king's mercy. There was a dispute between the barons and the bishops over which of them should pronounce sentence, the former saying that an ecclesiastic ought to be judged by their own, the latter insisting that this was a secular judgement and therefore should fall on the barons. Eventually, on the king's orders, the bishop of Winchester pronounced sentence, and all the bishops except for Gilbert of London agreed to stand surety for Thomas. The king then brought forward John the Marshal's accusation that he had not been given justice in the archbishop's court. Thomas argued that John had not made his case (nor had he turned up), and the king decided not to press the point. Here John the Marshal drops out of the story. Within the year he lost a son, and the following year John himself died, all of which Thomas attributed to divine judgement.[5]

Another of John's sons would in time become much more famous than his father: William Marshal, first earl of Pembroke, would serve five kings and gain a reputation as the greatest chivalric hero of his age.

Later that day King Henry pressed the archbishop further. He claimed that Thomas had received £300 as chancellor from revenues accruing from his custody of two royal castles, and demanded that he pay it back. Thomas protested, but agreed to return the money to the king. The next day the king demanded that Thomas repay money he had borrowed as chancellor, including a loan incurred in the expedition to Toulouse in 1159, and also called him to account for the revenues that he had handled when he had taken into his custody on the king's behalf vacant abbacies and bishoprics. This has been reckoned at £30,000 in total over the seven years of his chancellorship.[6] Thomas said that he had not been summoned to answer on these charges, and that he was prepared to make answer at the right place and time, but that he needed to consult with his bishops and clerks.

The next day the clergy came to his lodgings offering conflicting advice. Some urged him to appease the king by offering money. Others advised him to submit himself entirely to the king's mercy, among them Hilary, bishop of Chichester, who said, 'If only you could be not archbishop but just Thomas.'[7] Hilary claimed that the king had declared that there was no way that the two of them could remain in England with him as king and Thomas as archbishop. Therefore, the choice was for Thomas to resign his office or else to suffer imprisonment or violence. But another of the bishops said, on the contrary, that this was not a moment for Thomas to think of his own safety, for 'none of his predecessors did so, though they suffered persecution in their time.'[8] The next day too was given over entirely to such discussions and Thomas did not leave his lodgings. On the sixth day Thomas suddenly fell ill. He trembled with cold

and pain, and warm pillows had to be applied repeatedly, but he
sent a message to the king that he would come to court the next
day if his health permitted.

For days Thomas had been on the defensive, as the king used
a combination of public humiliation, legal manoeuvre and
threats to intimidate and isolate the archbishop. Now on Tuesday,
13 October, Thomas began to take up some of his own weapons.
That morning he received in his lodgings the bishops of London,
Winchester and Salisbury who had been sent by the king to
demand that he submit to judgement in his court. Thomas responded by forbidding the bishops, under his authority as their
metropolitan, from judging him in the king's court, and by
announcing that he was appealing to the pope against their judgement. He also ordered the bishops to loose ecclesiastical censures
against anyone who should lay violent hands on him. What
Thomas did here was not only an act of defence, but a violation
of the Constitutions of Clarendon, which had sanctioned the
trial of clerics in the king's court and prohibited appeals to the
pope without the king's licence. Bishop Gilbert of London in
response announced that he was appealing to the pope against
Thomas, thus beginning the series of appeals and counter-
appeals to the pope that would continue for another six years.

The bishops withdrew and Thomas went to say Mass. Nothing
unusual about that, except for the Mass that Thomas chose to
celebrate. For instead of marking the feast of a saint on the calendar for that day, Thomas chose to say the Mass of St Stephen
– the first Christian martyr, who had faced trial before the secular authorities before suffering death for Christ. It included the
hymn, 'For princes sat, and spoke against me, and they have
persecuted me unjustly.'⁹ If this was not pointed enough, the
Mass that he might have been expected to celebrate that day was
one in honour of St Edward the Confessor, Henry II's forebear
whose translation had been celebrated at Westminster Abbey

in the presence of king and archbishop a year ago to the day. Instead of celebrating a symbol of saintly and religious English kingship, Thomas associated himself with a martyr of the Church who had been tried and persecuted by the secular power.

According to one account, Thomas wished to proceed to the council chamber wearing his vestments but was dissuaded from doing so.[10] Nonetheless, he presented an equally striking spectacle when he entered the hall where the bishops were assembled, for just before he did so he took the large processional cross from the hands of his cross-bearer and carried it in his own hands before him. In fitz Stephen's account, one of Thomas's own clerks, shocked at this provocative act, appealed to Gilbert of London to take the cross from the archbishop's hands, to which Gilbert replied, 'My good man, he was always a fool and always will be.'[11] But Edward Grim has Gilbert trying, unsuccessfully, to wrestle the cross from Thomas's hands. Grim also relates how Roger, archbishop of York, said to Thomas, 'You enter armed against the lord king, but you can be sure that the king's sword cuts sharply, and it has already been drawn against you, unless you act more prudently.' Thomas in reply said, 'I know that the king's sword cuts, but it only cuts the flesh. The cross pierces the very soul and cuts through spiritual powers.'[12]

Thomas's action in carrying the cross, and the exchange it prompted, are full of significance, but they only make sense in the context of theological discussions of the day. Though obscure today, one of the most common ways of conceptualizing temporal and spiritual power in the twelfth century was to speak about them as 'two swords'. The image derives from a passage in Luke's gospel, where the disciples said to Jesus, 'Look, Lord, here are two swords,' and Jesus replied, 'It is enough.'[13] Medieval theorists interpreted this as a reference to the worldly or 'temporal' power of kings and princes on the one hand, and the spiritual power of the Church and its priests on the other. This

was in part a recognition of two spheres of influence, often dis-
tinct in rights and objectives. These spheres were not necessarily
in conflict, though since the time of Pope Gregory vii and the
Investiture Controversy, intellectuals within the Church had
developed arguments for the superiority of the spiritual sword
over the temporal sword. Herbert of Bosham has Thomas speaking in these terms to the king at the Council of Westminster a
year earlier:

> My lord king, holy church, the mother of all, both secular
> and priestly, has two kings, two laws, two jurisdictions
> and two types of punishment: two kings, Christ the King
> of Heaven and the worldly king; two laws, human and
> divine; two jurisdictions, priestly and lay; two types of
> punishment, spiritual and worldly. 'Behold there are
> two swords.' 'It is sufficient,' said the Lord.

The clergy, continued Thomas, are set apart from the rest of
society and given over specially to the work of the Lord, and
hence they are not subject to but superior to earthly kings.[14]
But there is another, related, aspect to the doctrine of the
two swords. Churchmen did not wield the temporal sword, for
they were excluded from involvement in any physical force.
Worldly powers were supposed to use the sword for the protection of the Church and people, for in some cases violent coercion
was necessary. And physical violence was an everyday part of
judgement in medieval England. Those who transgressed against
the laws of King Henry ii were liable to imprisonment, hanging,
mutilation and other penalties. At one point on this final day
of the Council of Northampton, a group of nobles were heard
to mutter loudly within earshot of the archbishop of how Henry's
ancestors had used physical violence against churchmen too.
Remember, they said, how William the Conqueror had arrested

and imprisoned his bishops, and how Henry II's own father, Geoffrey of Anjou, had ordered the castration of one of his Norman bishops who had dishonoured him.[15] These were real punishments that might await Thomas and any churchmen or lay nobles who supported him.

In this atmosphere of violence, what weapons did Thomas have? Here is where we see the significance of Thomas carrying his cross. Of course, this act symbolizes Thomas's association of himself with Christ and the cause of the Church, as Jesus said, 'If any man will come after me, let him deny himself, and take up his cross, and follow me.'[16] But also, the processional cross that Thomas held in his hands was the one presented to him by a papal delegation when he became archbishop, symbolizing his powers of jurisdiction. In other words, it showed that Thomas himself held the 'spiritual sword', by which he could coerce the sons of the Church. In particular it meant the weapons of excommunication (exclusion from the sacraments and rites of the Church) and interdict (prohibition on the performance of sacraments and rites). It showed that he was ready to use such measures, and that whereas the king's sword could only cut through the flesh, the archbishop's sword could pierce the spirit.[17]

While the bishops went to speak to the king, rumours spread through the archbishop's party that Thomas would that day be either imprisoned or would be violently attacked by a conspiracy of evil men. Herbert of Bosham told Thomas that should anyone lay impious hands upon him, he could immediately excommunicate them. But fitz Stephen, who was sitting at the archbishop's feet, urged him instead to follow the example of the apostles and martyrs, to pray for his persecutors and remain patient. When the bishops informed the king that Thomas had appealed to the pope against their judging him, he sent his clerks and barons to ask Thomas if this was true, and if he would provide guarantees for bail and stand judgement on rendering accounts of his chancellorship. Thomas, says fitz Stephen, 'looking at the image of the Crucified, firm in mind and countenance, and remaining seated, so as to preserve his dignity as archbishop', answered calmly and evenly, without halting in one word.[18] Yes, he said, he was bound to the king by homage, fealty and oath, but by his priestly oath he was obliged to preserve obedience to God, ecclesiastical dignity and the honour of his own office. He insisted that he had not been summoned to render accounts for his time as chancellor, that his appointment as archbishop had made him exempt from all such secular claims, and that he could not call on any more friends to provide sureties. As for the appeal, he declared that this was warranted on account of how unfairly he had been judged in the case of John the Marshal, and he concluded by saying, 'I place my person and the Canterbury church under the protection of God and the lord pope.'[19]

At this defiant statement one of the king's men was heard to say, 'Behold the blasphemy of prohibition that we have heard from his mouth!' – the words of the High Priest condemning Jesus in Matthew's gospel.[20] Some of the bishops, too, turned angrily on the archbishop. Hilary of Chichester complained that Thomas had placed them 'between the hammer and the anvil', forced to choose between disobeying his prohibition on judging him, and disobeying the king's customs.[21] And therefore, on this account, and also to prevent him from adding any further injury, the bishops appealed in turn to the pope against Thomas. To this Thomas replied he had only agreed to the king's customs with reservations, and besides, 'If we lapsed at Clarendon (for the flesh is weak), we ought to regain our spirit, and in the strength of the Holy Spirit rise up against the ancient enemy'[22] – that is, the Devil.

Now came the moment for Thomas's judgement in the upper room. On account of their appeal to the pope, the bishops were allowed to excuse themselves from the proceedings, so Thomas was judged by the earls, barons and some royal officials. What precisely Thomas was convicted of is not clear. He may have been declared guilty of treason, and condemned for failing to submit accounts for his time as chancellor.[23] The reason that we do not know is that sentence was never given. Robert earl of Leicester was entrusted with delivering the sentence on behalf of the other nobles, but uncomfortable with the task, he first tried to excuse himself and then entered upon a long rehearsal of what had occurred at the Council of Clarendon. Eventually Thomas would hear no more, and reportedly said, 'What is it that you wish to do? Have you come to judge me?' – the words of Jesus to the tribunal. 'On this you cannot judge me,' he continued. 'I am your father; you are nobles of the palace, lay potentates, secular persons. I will not hear your judgement.' The nobles withdrew, and after an interval the archbishop rose and, carrying his cross, approached the door. He passed through the crowd as one called him a perjurer, another a traitor, and on the way stumbled over a bundle of firewood but did not fall. When Thomas and his clerks reached the gate, the pressure of the crowds was so great that Herbert could not get on his own horse quickly enough and had to jump onto Thomas's as it rode away from the castle. 'O what a martyrdom in spirit he bore that day!', writes fitz Stephen, 'But he returned more happily from the council, because he was held worthy there to suffer insult for Jesus' name.'[24]

Escape

Back at their lodgings at St Andrew's Priory that evening, some of the clerks and laymen in his employ approached the archbishop and asked to be released from his service, a sign if any was needed of his disgrace before the king. Thomas, in an echo of the gospel parable of the rich man's supper, called in some of the poor and had them take the place of the departed at his table. During dinner the archbishop's party received a sign of another kind.

Herbert says that the pious reading during the meal quoted Christ's instruction to his apostles, 'When they persecute you in one city, flee to the next.' As they heard these words, Thomas and his disciple looked up and their eyes met.[25] Certainly, in Thomas's mind, he was facing persecution, and remaining in England presented few opportunities and much danger. But it was not an easy step for an archbishop of Canterbury to flee the land. The Constitutions of Clarendon stated quite explicitly, 'Archbishops, bishops and beneficed clergy may not leave the realm without the king's licence. And if they shall leave, if it pleases the king, they shall give security that neither in going nor in staying nor in returning shall they promote evil or damage to the lord king or the realm.'[26] It was on these grounds that King Henry would later charge Thomas with fleeing like a traitor. Not only that, but canon law prohibited senior ecclesiastics from 'fleeing from city to city' except in the strictest circumstances. Archbishops and bishops who fled persecution, even if such persecution was indisputable, could be accused of abandoning the flocks committed to them. As Jesus said in the gospel, 'I am the good shepherd. The good shepherd lays down his life for the sheep. He who is a hireling and not the shepherd, whose own the sheep are not, sees the wolf coming and leaves the sheep and flees.'[27]

But Thomas also had precedents for the action that he was now planning. Archbishop Anselm had gone into exile first on account of his disputes with King William II, and again during the reign of Henry I. Archbishop Theobald had sailed to France against the prohibition of King Stephen, and Thomas his clerk had gone with him. Thomas's supporters claimed that in fleeing he was following the example of St Paul and Jesus himself, who on occasion retreated from danger, thereby preserving themselves for more fruitful action on behalf of the Church. That night, Thomas ordered his bed to be brought into the

church and placed behind the high altar, and stationed a servant
nearby to prevent anyone from approaching. Then, when night
fell, Thomas summoned two lay brethren from his retinue and
a loyal personal servant and arranged for horses to be brought up
to the door of the house. Their escape from the town was aided
by the darkness of the night, and by torrential rain, which kept
the townspeople indoors and muffled the sounds of the horses'
hooves, and they were able to make their way through the northern gate of the city, which they found unguarded. With day
approaching they reached Lincoln, where they lodged with a
friend. The king's words on hearing of Thomas's flight were said
to be, 'We are not finished with this fellow yet.' But although
he had all the shores of the sea watched, he ordered that none
of the archbishop's property was to be touched, the better to em-
phasize the king's clemency and the archbishop's recklessness.

Twelfth-century England had a system of roads, some dating
back to Roman times, that supported an increasing number of
soldiers, traders, pilgrims and other travellers on the move. But
Thomas and his men made a circuitous route to the southeast
coast, using lonely paths and waterways, travelling by night and
relying on a network of friends. Eventually they reached Eastry
on the Kent coast, a manor belonging to the Canterbury monks
where Thomas hid for eight days. A little before daybreak on
2 November, Thomas embarked in a skiff without any baggage,
and that evening landed on the coast of Flanders, not far from
the port of Gravelines.[28] On the night that Thomas fled from
Northampton, a member of his household, unaware of the flight,
is said to have heard in his sleep a voice chanting the lines of
the psalm, 'Safe, like a bird rescued from the fowler's snare; the
snare is broken and we are safe.' But Thomas still had to pass
through the lands of the count of Flanders and his brother, the
count of Boulogne, neither of whom was sympathetic to him.
Herbert describes how the sorry group of exiles made their way

along the muddy and slippery road from the Flemish coast to
their intended destination at St Bertin. Unable to proceed any
further on foot, the brethren purchased a packhorse for a shil-
ling, and had the archbishop sit upon it. Herbert breaks out into
rapturous celebration of Thomas's new circumstances:

> What a sight to see Thomas, once on chariots and
> horses, now astride a packhorse, with only a halter
> around its neck for a bridle and the rags of the poor
> brothers and lay brothers on its back for a saddle!
> What a change of circumstances, Thomas! Where
> are all those horses and knights you used to have,
> all those rich and ostentatious trappings? Look at
> all these now reduced to one packhorse and one
> halter, and not even your packhorse or halter but
> another's. As you change, the things belonging to
> you also change, as your old things pass away and
> all become new.[29]

Even in these changed circumstances, Thomas struggled to con-
ceal his identity. Though he had changed his name to 'Christian',
and disguised himself in the habit of a lay brother, he was recognized by the keeper of an inn where the exiles stopped. The
innkeeper was struck by how this guest distributed food to
others from his own plate, and also noticed the man's build and
posture, his height, large brow and serious expression, hand-
some face, long hands and elegant fingers, and sensed that he
was in the presence of someone great, perhaps the archbishop of
Canterbury. Another time, Thomas drew unwarranted attention
to himself when he stopped to examine a falcon that a young
knight was holding on his wrist.[30] After another stay in hiding
in a hermitage surrounded by water, he reached the abbey of St
Bertin, the place where Anselm and Theobald had both stayed

Thomas Becket welcomed by the French king, 13th century, stained glass, Chartres Cathedral.

during exile, where he was reunited with Herbert of Bosham. From there Thomas was given an escort out of Flanders and into the territories of the king of France.

Earlier that year, when John of Salisbury went into exile in France, he wrote to Thomas that from the moment he landed on that side of the Channel he thought he felt a gentler breeze: 'As the storms of calamity subside, I have been astonished and delighted to find everywhere prosperity, and a peaceful and content folk.'³¹ Herbert of Bosham would write even more exuberantly, 'Sweet France, truly sweet is she . . . her people have made drunken with delight all those that came to her, with the cup of her sweetness.'³² Thomas would spend all but one month of the last six years of his life in France, and for most of that time he was able to rely on the support of King Louis and the French Church. Louis had known Thomas since at least 1158 when he had warmly welcomed the chancellor's embassy to Paris. He had a reputation for piety, and had been an enthusiastic if ineffective crusader, leading a disastrous expedition to the Holy Land in 1147. King Louis also, of course, had a history of tension with King Henry, and that king's troubles with his archbishop could be turned to his own advantage.

But none of this meant that Louis would automatically offer his support to Thomas, and it was King Henry's envoys who reached him first at his court at Compiègne. There they presented him with a letter in the name of their king, which stated that Thomas had fled the realm as a traitor, and begged Louis not to receive him in his land. But when Louis saw that the letter referred to 'Thomas, formerly archbishop of Canterbury', he asked the envoys who had deposed him. 'Certainly, like the king of England, I am also a king,' he said. 'Nonetheless I do not have the power to depose the lowliest clerk in my kingdom.' The English mission departed with little encouragement and the next day Herbert of Bosham and a companion arrived at Compiègne and received a much warmer welcome. The exiles recounted their adventures and troubles, and Louis reported his interview with the English embassy. The king offered his peace and protection to Thomas as long as he should remain in his kingdom, noting that it had long been a tradition of the kingdom of France to provide hospitality to exiles, especially ecclesiastics. Soon after this King Louis came to Soissons where he met Thomas, reiterated this assurance to him and provided him with financial support.[33]

The next step was to solicit the support of Pope Alexander and the papal curia, and to this end the royal envoys made their way to the city of Sens, and Thomas's envoys followed in their footsteps a day behind them.[34] First, on 26 November 1164 the king's envoys made their case, in the presence of the pope, the cardinals and the archbishop's envoys. It was an impressive embassy, including the archbishop of York and five bishops, as well as earls and barons. First to speak was Gilbert of London, who accused Thomas of relying on his own wisdom, and seeking to disturb the peace of the Church and devotion to the king. 'Recently,' he said, 'for a trivial and unimportant reason, a conflict has arisen in England between the crown and the priesthood which could have been avoided had a restrained approach been taken.' But Thomas, following his own counsel alone, took too vigorous a stand, 'not considering the evil of the time, or the danger that could result'. Then, said Gilbert, 'with no one using force or even making threats he took to flight, as is written, "The wicked man flees, when no one is pursuing".' At this the pope interrupted and rebuked Gilbert for his strong language, and the bishop became so confused that he could not mutter another word. Next Hilary of Chichester called on the pope to intervene, 'lest the obstinacy of one man be allowed to wreak havoc on many'. But Hilary, a man often noted for his eloquence, made an unaccustomed grammatical mistake in Latin (mixing up the imperfect with the perfect tense), causing the assembly to dissolve in laughter. The most effective speech was by a layman, William, earl of Arundel, who spoke in French. He reminded the pope how King Henry had remained faithful to him since the start of the schism, but he also praised the archbishop's ability and prudence, even if he could be 'a little too sharp'. Were it not for the present dispute, he said, 'crown and priesthood would rejoice together in mutual peace and concord under a good ruler and an excellent pastor', and he begged the pope to strive attentively for peace.[35]

The envoys had sought to persuade the pope to send a delegation to England to judge on the dispute there, hoping that it would decide in the king's favour. But the pope insisted that final judgement should be reserved for himself, and the embassy departed in frustration. A few days later Thomas arrived at Sens, and he was called to present his case before the pope. Although he had many learned men with him, they all excused themselves, letting the burden fall on Thomas himself, though his poor spoken Latin and his stammer are attested by contemporaries. Drawing a contrast between the downfall of the king's envoys who possessed worldly eloquence but not virtue or truth, Alan of Tewkesbury says that Thomas spoke, 'not prepared by himself but instructed by God'. The archbishop began by drawing attention to the loss of honour and security that he had incurred in disputing with the king and fleeing into exile, but insisted that he had to do so on account of his profession. Then he presented the Constitutions before the assembly, saying, 'See what the king of England has set up against the liberty of the Catholic Church.' When the Constitutions were read through, everyone was moved to tears, and even those who had first opposed Thomas now agreed that they must come to the aid of the universal Church in the person of the archbishop.[36]

The next day Thomas attended a private meeting with the pope and cardinals. There he laid the blame for the dispute on himself. 'I confess that my wretched fault brought these troubles upon the English Church,' he said. He had been appointed archbishop not by canonical election, but through the pressure of the royal power: 'What wonder then, if it turned out badly for me?' And then Thomas dramatically resigned his office into the hands of the pope. Though Thomas's men were reportedly aghast at this, Thomas's gesture had a useful purpose. After some consultation with the cardinals, the pope spoke about how dangerous a precedent it would be for a prelate to be deposed for protecting the Church's liberty. And concluding that Thomas was 'fighting the battle of us all', he restored him fully

Thomas Becket meeting Pope Alexander III, miniature from a manuscript of Vincent of Beauvais, *Speculum historiale*, 1459–63.

to his office, thereby removing any taint that might attach to him on account of his original appointment.[37] Pope Alexander's approach throughout the dispute could be described positively as a balanced one, or more negatively as vacillating. He tended to match support for the archbishop's cause with measures designed to restrain him from overly vigorous action, and his policy in November 1164 was no different. At the same time as he restored Thomas to office and encouraged him in his fight for the Church's cause, he also dispatched him to a place where he might cause minimal trouble to the king. Thomas, said the pope, had hitherto delighted in riches but now he ought to learn to be a comforter of the poor, and the only way to do that was to learn poverty for himself. Therefore, Alexander announced that he had arranged for Thomas and his companions to be sent for training to the abbey of Pontigny: 'Not, I say, to be trained in splendour but in simplicity, as befits an exile and an athlete of Christ.'[38]

Retreat and Resurgence

Pontigny owed its existence to a movement for reform that swept through the western Church in the late eleventh and early twelfth century when men and women increasingly came to express a desire for a more austere form of life, one closer to that they imagined the early apostles had lived. In 1098 a new monastery was founded at Cîteaux, near Dijon, by a group of monks who were seeking a more rigorous life than that pursued at the old Benedictine monasteries or at the newer Cluniac houses. By 1113 the community at Cîteaux had grown sufficiently that they founded a new house at La Ferté, and the following year the second 'daughter house', Pontigny, was established. Over the following decades the Cistercian Order, taking its name from their first foundation, would spread rapidly throughout Europe,

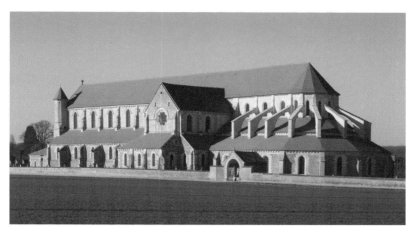

Pontigny Abbey.

including many houses in England. The driving force was Bernard
of Clairvaux, whose theology, preaching and intervention in
affairs of state made him one of the dominant figures in the
twelfth-century Church. By the time Thomas entered Pontigny,
it was a well-established and highly respected institution, pat-
ronized by kings and nobles, and linked to the other Cistercian
houses through a corporate structure. But Pontigny had not lost
the distinctive way of life for which it had been founded. Like
other Cistercian houses, it was located in a wilderness, in dense
forest, some distance from urban life. There the monks, in their
distinctive garb of undyed wool, eschewed ornamentation in
favour of simple church buildings, and rejected all luxuries in
favour of simple food and manual labour.[39]

Herbert of Bosham was among the group that accompanied
Thomas to Pontigny, and he says that there they immediately
began to direct themselves to the pursuit of a new, reformed life.
This, says Herbert, was the time that Thomas had always longed
for, the time 'when now at last he might make up for the loss of
squandered days', so that even if belatedly, he would learn how
to rule over himself, and thus rule over others. That monastery

was, Herbert says, 'like a training school for combat, in which we were exercised together, a school of virtue in which we were educated together'. He and others claim that, although the exiles were not required to follow the full rigours of the Cistercian life, Thomas surpassed all others in his asceticism. He restricted his diet to vegetables and coarser foods, secretly distributing delicacies to the indigent. One source claims that Thomas joined the other monks in agricultural labour. Others tell of him standing up to his neck in a freezing cold stream, purging his desires. Herbert says that he had to dissuade Thomas from going too far in his ascetic practices, fearing that they would irreparably damage his health.[40] Many of these stories bear suspicious similarities to tales of other saintly ascetics, from Benedict of Nursia to Godric of Finchale, and like the claims about the hairshirt and Thomas's mortifications upon becoming archbishop they are difficult to verify. Yet there is no doubt that the move to Pontigny brought Thomas into an environment very different to that to which he was accustomed.

Another new feature of Thomas's life at Pontigny was his embrace of spiritual study. Herbert says that after all his troubles, Thomas began to turn himself entirely to reading, prayer and meditation. After he had completed the regular hours – the round of prayers that structured the day for Cistercian monks – the sacred books would hardly leave his hands for the whole day, especially the Psalms and Epistles, 'like two spiritual eyes', from which he would learn mystic contemplation and ethics. Herbert himself was working on a commentary on these two books of the Bible, and he acted as Thomas's instructor in the Scriptures, though he claims that Thomas made so much progress so quickly that he would soon become the true teacher. During this time Thomas also began to study law, taught by Lombard of Piacenza, an expert in both civil and canon law. When John of Salisbury heard about this he wrote to the archbishop advising him to put away the study of law and other activities, and instead to devote himself to the contemplation of the Psalms, and Gregory the Great's commentary on the book of Job.[41] At Pontigny Thomas certainly had time to reflect on his suffering and to call out to God to protect him, in the mode of Job and the Psalmist, but events in the world outside did not cease while he was in retreat. And when he had the opportunity, Thomas would again revive from his repose to take vigorous action on behalf of the Church.

While the exiles were settling in at Pontigny, King Henry had begun to take reprisals. At his Christmas court at Marlborough in December 1164 he ordered that Thomas be deprived of all his possessions, and that the church of Canterbury including all its lands, be forfeited to the crown. He committed these to Ranulf de Broc, doorkeeper of the king's chamber, royal brothel-keeper and one of those who had shouted abuse at Thomas at Northampton. The archbishop's clerks, too, were to have their churches and revenues confiscated. Furthermore, all of the archbishop's relatives and the clerks and laymen of his household were to be deprived and banished from the kingdom. William fitz Stephen describes in pitiful detail how this 'tattered procession' of men and women, with infants in cradles or clinging to the breast, were all ordered from their home and crossed the sea. To make these expulsions even more bitter to Thomas, the banished were ordered to make their way to the archbishop himself at Pontigny, though in fact many were given hospitality by the king, nobles and churches of France. In a further outrage, the king prohibited his subjects from providing any aid to the archbishop, including their prayers.[42]

Thomas had few options available to him in 1165 apart from endurance. Attempts to win over influential figures to his side, including the king's mother Matilda, bore little fruit, and the pope was careful to keep him on a firm leash. Though Alexander felt secure enough in his position to end his French exile and return to Italy in April of that year, he soon began to hear disturbing reports of diplomatic exchanges between the king of England and the emperor of Germany. Recently the archbishop of Cologne had visited England, and when he returned to Germany he was accompanied by two of King Henry's clerks – John of Oxford and Richard of Ilchester – who joined in an oath to renounce Pope Alexander and recognize the new antipope, Paschal. That summer, the pope sent letters into England warning the king to reinstate Thomas to his office and not to waver in his support for the true pope, and Henry did in fact soon retreat from his flirtation with the schismatics. Yet Alexander still saw danger, as can be seen from his letter to Thomas in summer 1165:

> Since the days are evil, and many things must be tolerated because of the times, we request your discretion. We advise, counsel and urge you, that in everything you do regarding your own affairs and those of the Church, you show yourself cautious, prudent and circumspect, and do nothing hastily or precipitately, but act seasonably and responsibly, and strive in every way possible to recover the favour and goodwill of the illustrious king of England, as much as can be done saving the liberty of the Church and the honour of your office.

Until the following Easter, the pope continued, Thomas should take care not to act against the king or his lands, 'For then the Lord will grant us better days, and both you and we will be able to proceed in this business with greater security.'[43]

Herbert suggests that, some time before Easter 1166, Thomas had already decided that their time of repose and retreat should come to an end. Realizing how hardened were the hearts of his enemies, he says, the archbishop began to meditate on how best to respond. He considered his duty as a priest to stand up zealously in defence of justice, but he also thought about his

duty as a spiritual father. A loving father sometimes needs to
show compassion to an errant son, but in other cases he must
punish iniquities with the rod and sins with lashes. 'Up to now
we have been silent, but does that mean that we will always be
silent?', he asked his companions. 'We, who up to now have slept
in solitude between these monks and these stones, do we not

Barbarossa the Crusader, miniature from *Historia Hierosolymitana*,
c. 1188.

also awake?'[44] His first step was to send three letters in succession to King Henry, warning him to change his ways. Each letter was more severe in its warning, and the final letter was delivered to the king by a 'squalid monk'. Filled with allusions to the Bible and early Christian writers, intellectually these letters clearly owe much to the expertise of his learned advisors. But as a gesture, they have all the hallmarks of Thomas himself.[45]

In these letters Thomas addresses the relationship between the two powers, and the damage to ecclesiastical liberties that the king has inflicted. The Church, he says, includes two orders. The clergy, who include the apostles, popes, bishops and others, are given rule over the Church, so that they may direct everything towards the salvation of souls. The people, among whom are kings, princes and other potentates, conduct secular affairs for the benefit of the peace and security of the Church. And since kings receive their power from the Church, and the Church receives hers from Christ,

> you do not have the power to command bishops to
> absolve or excommunicate anyone, to draw clergy
> to secular judgements, to pass judgement concerning
> churches and tithes, to forbid bishops to hear cases
> concerning breach of faith or oaths, and many other
> things of this kind, which are written down among
> your customs, which you call 'ancestral'.[46]

But as well as stating the case for ecclesiastical liberty, Thomas is quick to remind the king of the pastor's duty of correction. To speak freely to a king may provoke the king's anger, but yet it is for his benefit that he speaks. For Henry is not only his lord and king, but his spiritual son, and thus Thomas has a responsibility to reprove him when he transgresses. Thomas reminds Henry of the example of the biblical king David, who humbled himself and recovered God's favour all the more abundantly. Other kings who refused to mend their ways, such as Pharaoh and Saul, suffered terrible retribution. God gave power of judgement over the clergy to bishops and priests, not to worldly powers, and there are many cases in history of priests judging kings. And should Henry not follow the example of the penitent David, Thomas will have no option but to cry out, 'Avenge, O Lord, the sufferings of your servants.'[47]

King Henry and those around him may not have given much thought to these arguments, but they would have understood what these letters portended. They would have recognized the threefold warning, each letter more strict in its message than the last, as the standard prelude to excommunication. This was the pattern recommended in the Bible and followed by ecclesiastical leaders from St Ambrose in the fourth century to Pope Gregory VII in the late eleventh century, when they decided to take action against recalcitrant rulers. In short, it was Thomas's announcement that he was preparing to unsheathe the spiritual sword. On 24 April 1166 Pope Alexander appointed Thomas papal legate in England (though he exempted the province of York from this authority), giving him powers to issue sentences of excommunication and interdict in the pope's name. He directed Thomas 'not to defer exercising ecclesiastical justice when you consider it opportune' against those who had done violence or injury to the archbishop, his people and his properties.[48] Pope Alexander evidently hoped that King Henry might be more responsive to appeals for peace knowing that Thomas held this powerful weapon of coercion. He may not have expected him to use it so quickly.

FIVE

Thomas Alone

A certain image recurs throughout his life of Thomas alone in a crowd. As a young man he is said to have joined in the ribald conversation of his fellows while secretly keeping his mind on higher things. As chancellor he is presented as concealing a deeper spiritual purpose beneath his lavish clothes, a phenomenon that became sharpened on his elevation as archbishop when he began to wear a hairshirt and monastic garb, hidden from all but his closest confidants. Abandoned by the bishops at Northampton, he fled to France with a handful of companions. In exile he often appeared to stand alone against the Church's enemies as he was assailed by his episcopal colleagues, betrayed by the papal curia and undermined by his former friends. The final image of Thomas, and the most famous, is of him standing with head bowed, surrounded by the swords of his murderers.

Thomas lived his life surrounded by others, but he often cut an isolated figure. This is especially so in the last years of his life, 1167 to 1170. During these years the dispute that began with a clash between king and archbishop came to draw in more and more people, with diverse and often conflicting interests. These included the English episcopacy, which harboured shades of opinion, and found itself placed in an especially difficult position by the hostility between king and archbishop. The pope and the cardinals had reasons for supporting Thomas, but also reasons to fear the king, as did the monks of Canterbury, and even within Thomas's closest circles there could be differences. Thomas's isolation was one of the main charges made against him by his critics. He was seen as standing apart from his fellow churchmen, and indeed from his saintly predecessors in office. Instead of following the wise counsel of others, he pursued his own path, to the point where he alienated even his strongest supporters. And when people try to understand Thomas's character, this is often how he appears most of all – as a loner. But isolation could also be praised by Thomas's supporters, who claimed that he was following the lonely path of truth and justice. And in the light of the martyrdom it could be argued that the multitude was misguided, and he alone could see.

Thomas Against the Bishops

In late spring 1166 Thomas left Pontigny to make a pilgrimage to Soissons. There he spent three nights in prayer before the altars of the Virgin and St Gregory, the founder of the English Church, and before the tomb of St Drausius, a local saint who had a reputation for interceding on behalf of those who were about to face combat.[1] Then he travelled south to Vézelay, the place where twenty years before Bernard of Clairvaux had preached the sermon that launched the Second Crusade. On Whit Sunday, 12 June, at the invitation of the abbot, Thomas celebrated a public Mass in the abbey. There he delivered a fiery sermon in which he set out the cause of the conflict, complained of his mistreatment and that of his people, and the inflexibility of the king. Then suddenly, to the surprise of all, he announced the excommunication of John of Oxford and Richard of Ilchester for associating with schismatics, Bishop Jocelin of Salisbury for allowing John of Oxford's uncanonical appointment as dean of Salisbury, the royal servants Richard de Luci and Jocelin de

Balliol for their treatment of the English Church, and Ranulf de
Broc and others for usurping Canterbury possessions.[2]

There are two puzzling aspects to Thomas's actions at Vézelay.
One is that, according to Herbert, Thomas's companions were
entirely taken by surprise, believing that the archbishop had
come to Vézelay to celebrate the approaching feast of St Mary
Magdalene.[3] But the recent award of the legation, combined
with the tenor of the letters to Henry II, strongly suggest that
the exiles expected Thomas to take strong measures against his
enemies, even if he had not revealed to them the exact time
and place. Then there is the question of why, after such clearly
stated threats, Thomas recoiled from censuring the king himself
or laying an interdict on his lands. John of Salisbury said that
Thomas chose to omit the king from his censures because he
heard he had fallen ill.[4] But it should also be considered that,
although Thomas has often been accused of rashness for his
actions at Vézelay, he was enough of a tactician to foresee the
outrage that more severe measures against the king might provoke at this point. Even more so, he might have appreciated the
value of keeping this weapon in reserve.

Excommunication was a grave punishment, but the sentence
of excommunication required not only that it be issued but that
it be observed, and Henry II had various means by which he might
thwart the implementation of Thomas's censures. First he had
the ports watched to prevent Thomas's letters of censure from
reaching their recipients, and when this was unsuccessful he
sought to forestall their imposition with appeals to the pope. To
this end he summoned the bishops and abbots of the realm to a
council in London on 24 June, where the clergy of the province
of Canterbury appealed to the pope against Thomas's sentences,[5]
and also wrote a letter of complaint to Thomas himself.

The Vézelay sentences provoked a barrage of correspondence between Thomas and his clerks on the one hand and

critical bishops on the other. These letters are manifestos, backed
by references to the Bible, the writings of the Church Fathers
and canon law, and designed to persuade and denounce. But for
all their rhetorical fireworks, they are also valuable statements
of position by various interests in the dispute, and particularly
the shades of opinion held by different churchmen. They also
illustrate the importance of letter-writing in the Becket dispute,
and more broadly in twelfth-century literate culture. From about
1166 Thomas and his household in exile had begun to make a
careful collection of their correspondence. Such a practice had
precedents, notably during the Investiture Controversy of the
late eleventh and early twelfth century when both the papal
and the imperial side collected their letters and circulated them
for propaganda purposes. Letter-writing flourished in the twelfth
century, and the Becket correspondence is among the best examples of it. Other letter collections of the period include those of
Bernard of Clairvaux, which range from theological medita-
tions to Crusade preaching, and those of Peter of Blois, a clerk
to Henry II, which veer between court gossip and reflections
on higher matters.[6] Some of the letters in Thomas's collection
are short and functional, reporting news or relaying an instruction. But others are works of art. Thomas surrounded himself
with educated men, who had studied rhetoric and were able
to deploy sophisticated techniques of argument, and some of his
opponents were just as skilled. In many cases, the important and
personal information was passed on by the bearer of the letter.
The letter itself was meant to be read aloud, to be circulated
beyond the recipient and to be appreciated for its language.

In the summer of 1166, at the same time as the clergy of
the province of Canterbury sent their appeal to the pope, they
wrote to Thomas, denouncing his recent actions. This letter
was immediately recognized as the work of Gilbert Foliot, but
it echoes views expressed elsewhere by many within the English

Thomas Becket pronouncing the sentence of excommunication
on his enemies, and arguing his case before Henry II and Louis VII
of France, miniature from the Becket Leaves, *c.* 1220–40.

episcopate who were by now despairing of their archbishop
and fearful of what would come next. The bishops write that
they had initially been pleased to hear that Thomas in his exile
had turned to prayer, fasts and vigils, and was not planning any
schemes against the king. But now they hear to their dismay
that the archbishop had threatened excommunication or interdict against the king, and can find no way to seek peace on his
behalf 'as long as battle is being waged as if with a drawn sword'.
They remind Thomas of all the things that the king has done
for him, how 'he raised you up from poverty and received you
into his intimate favour' so that every part of his great dominions
was subject to the chancellor's power. Then he raised Thomas
to the position of archbishop, trusting that with his support he
would reign happily, but instead of security (*securitatem*), he found
a battleaxe (*securim*). If Thomas cannot be moved to humility
and love, perhaps, they suggest, he will consider what would
happen should the king withdraw his support for Pope Alexander
on account of his archbishop's provocation. They do not claim

that King Henry has never sinned, but insist that he is always ready to make amends. Placed on the throne by God, the king provides peace for the Church and people, and in order to do so he requires that the dignities traditionally rendered to his royal predecessors should be rendered to him. By what right or law, they ask, will the archbishop impose excommunication or interdict on such a Christian king? And the bishops conclude by announcing that they have appealed against the suspension and condemnation of the bishop of Salisbury and his dean.[7]

The stance taken by the bishops and the strong language used might appear surprising if we consider the dispute as one primarily contested between the crown and the Church. Their rationalization of the royal customs as part of a desire to bring peace to the realm, their praise of the king's devotion to the Church and his willingness to come to a reconciliation, suggest at least qualified approval of Henry II's position. Their criticism of the archbishop's measures against his enemies and their exhortations to turn to humility might seem to suggest that Thomas was upholding the rights of the Church too vigorously. Indeed Thomas replied to this letter with a lengthy condemnation of the bishops for their failure to stand with him. He had remained silent a long time, he writes, 'waiting to see if the Lord would perchance inspire you who turned your backs on the day of battle to recover your strength', but no one would rise to the fight. The conduct of the dispute, he says, is left to him alone as he cries out to God, 'Rise up, O Lord, judge your cause.'[8] But neither the bishops nor Thomas are discussing principle here as much as practice. For most of Thomas's ecclesiastical critics their concern was not so much that Thomas was an idealistic and vigorous defender of the Church. It was rather that his actions damaged the very cause that he claimed to uphold. The liberty of the Church required vigilance against usurpation, and this sometimes required the spiritual sword to be unsheathed against enemies of the Church. But the Church could not secure peace and liberty without pragmatism. There was a time for all things, a time for denunciation and vigorous action, but also a time for humility and moderation, and this was something that Thomas appeared unable to appreciate.[9]

There were also differences among the English bishops, who were driven by a range of motives, both principled and personal. Of all Thomas's critics, the sharpest was Gilbert Foliot, bishop of London.[10] Gilbert's background was very different from Thomas's. He was born into a noble family, and became a Cluniac monk, then prior and eventually abbot. In 1148 he was elected bishop of Hereford, and, though disappointed at being passed over for the archbishopric of Canterbury in favour of Thomas, he was transferred to the important see of London in 1163. Gilbert was also very different in temperament and interests. He did not eat meat or drink wine, and he was both an impressive preacher and a distinguished scholar. We have already seen how he was the lone voice of opposition to Thomas's election as archbishop, how he refused to stand surety for Thomas at Northampton and later rebuked him for carrying his cross into the chamber, and how he denounced Thomas at the papal court at Sens for provoking the king and putting his brethren in danger. In the summer of 1166, as well as responding to the bishops in general, Thomas wrote to the bishop of London expressing astonishment that a prudent, learned and religious man should openly oppose truth and justice and confuse right and wrong. Remember, he wrote, that we will all stand before the judgement seat of the strictest Judge: 'Truth alone will judge us.'[11] Gilbert responded with an elegant and devastating denunciation of Thomas. This famous letter, known as *Multiplicem nobis* from its opening words, presents not just an argument against the archbishop's actions, or a criticism of the man himself, but a skilful melding of the two. For Gilbert, matters could never go

right for the English Church when it was led by someone as
unsuitable as Thomas.

'It is difficult for things begun with bad beginnings to be
carried through to a good conclusion,' writes Gilbert, and central to his argument is the case that the root cause of the Church's
troubles lay in the elevation to archbishop of an unsuitable royal
servant. Before 1163, he claims, peace reigned between the two
powers: the crown respected the priesthood, and the priesthood
supported the king. But with Thomas's appointment disagree-
ments multiplied and hatred became entrenched. This was not,
he insists, because Thomas defended the rights of the Church
too vigorously, but rather because he was too weak in their
defence. While the bishops stood firm with their archbishop
through all the early disputes, it was their archbishop who abandoned them at Clarendon. 'Let the Lord judge between us,'
writes Gilbert, 'let him judge for whom we stood, for whom we
refused to give way before the threats of princes; let him judge
who fled, who was a deserter in the battle.' It was Thomas who
fled from righteousness by assenting to the king's customs. And
it was Thomas who then took to flight, escaping across the
Channel and leaving the bishops leaderless. Now with what gall
does he call on his brethren in England to suffer death for Christ?
'Yet it is not the pain that makes the martyr, but the cause,'
Gilbert reminds him. 'To suffer hardships religiously is an honourable thing: to suffer hardships wrongly and obstinately is dis-
honourable.' If battle is now joined with the king, Thomas will
safely escape it, but the English Church will not. And what is
this cause, Gilbert asks, for which we should be persuaded to
die? There is no dispute about the faith, about the sacraments
or concerning morals. It merely concerns those customs which
the king says had been rendered to his predecessors and he wishes
to be observed too in his time. When disputes arose in the past,
wise men succeeded in removing such customs, not by abuse or

threats but by blessing and preaching. Had Thomas followed the advice of his brethren and the prudent example of his predecessors, and weighed the Church's advantages and disadvantages, he might have gained more and averted destruction. Who considers it among a doctor's skills to cure one wound by inflicting another, far greater and more dangerous?[12] Gilbert's letter is influenced by thwarted ambition and personal antipathy, and it is a polished rhetorical argument rather than a balanced assessment of the facts. But there were surely many others within the English Church who shared the main sentiments expressed here: that Thomas's tainted character and means of assent made his failure as archbishop inevitable, and that while claiming to be a defender of the Church his actions instead left it dangerously open to destruction.

Thomas Against the World

In September 1166 King Henry took a further measure against Thomas. He complained to the Chapter General of the Cistercians that they were harbouring a public enemy, and that if they continued to do so he would confiscate the property of the Order in his dominions. Although the abbot of Pontigny protested, Thomas insisted that he did not wish the Cistercians to suffer through his fault. King Louis, fulfilling his promise to provide for the exiles, offered them a new place to settle just outside the city of Sens at the monastery of St Columbe. They would remain there for nearly four more years.[13] The period between Thomas's arrival at Sens in November 1166 and his reconciliation with the king in July 1170 is one of the most difficult to follow. It was a time of constant negotiation and diplomacy in search of peace, punctuated by measure and countermeasure by king and archbishop. It involved a great number of people, including Henry II's ministers and advocates, Thomas's clerks and supporters, King Louis, the pope and the cardinals, and many other ecclesiastics in England and France. During this time Pope Alexander returned to Italy, first to Rome before taking up residence further south in Benevento. Embassies from Thomas, Henry and some of the bishops travelled long distances between England, Italy and France, crossing paths with papal peace missions making their way between northern Europe and the Mediterranean. Herbert vividly describes how each side would send embassy upon embassy to the pope, 'wearing down the threshold of the apostles'.[14] Letters of appeal, instruction, admonition and confirmation were carried over distances of thousands of miles, so that the recipients could not be sure if the orders they received had in the meantime been countermanded or superseded. In this environment all parties listened carefully to intelligence reports and rumours, and acted to pre-empt the moves of their adversaries.

It is also important to consider that the pope, the kings of England and France, and the various ecclesiastics had many other cares besides the Becket dispute. And these cares, seemingly external to the conflict between Henry and Thomas, did much to shape the eventual peace terms and Thomas's return to England. In November 1166, just as the exiles were settling in at Sens, Frederick Barbarossa was in Lombardy with a large army and the following summer he was in Rome, where he had his wife crowned as empress by the antipope Paschal. This was a moment of great peril for Pope Alexander, who escaped south to Benevento. But just when the imperial army seemed triumphant, they were devastated by malaria and dysentery and were forced to retreat. This retreat, along with the strengthening of papal alliances in Italy and the death of the antipope in September 1168, saw Alexander's position strengthen, and with it his room for manoeuvre in the Becket dispute. Meanwhile, King Louis' staunch support for Thomas was on occasion undermined by the advantages of diplomacy with the king of England. But the most consequential factor for Thomas would be Henry II's determination that his son Henry would not suffer the problems of succession to the throne that his mother and he himself had faced. It was the coronation of the Young King in 1170 that broke the deadlock between king and archbishop, and it would also precipitate Thomas's murder.

Late in 1166 both archbishop and king sent missions to the pope, and it was the king's embassy that returned in triumph. The pope restored to office the excommunicate John of Oxford, one of the king's envoys, and at the same time he restrained Thomas from further action. To the archbishop he wrote:

> For this reason we ask, advise and counsel you as a
> prudent man, to bear with [the king] patiently until
> we can see the end and outcome of this affair, and
> you may not in the meanwhile decree anything against
> him, or anyone in his kingdom, which appears harsh
> or offensive to him.[15]

Not only that, but the pope announced that he was sending two cardinals as papal legates to settle the dispute, with powers to absolve those excommunicated by Thomas. When he heard the news, Gilbert Foliot reportedly exclaimed, 'Thomas will no longer be my archbishop.'[16] Cardinals Otto and William of Pavia arrived in northern France in autumn 1167, and visited the archbishop's party at Sens before going on to meet Henry II at Caen in Normandy. Then, on 18 November, they met with Thomas and his advisors at Planches on the frontier of Normandy. Herbert of Bosham says that the night before the conference Thomas had a dream in which he was given poison to drink in a golden cup, which put him on his guard against the honeyed speeches of William of Pavia. The cardinals told the exiles that the king was prepared to allow Thomas to return to Canterbury, but he could not countenance the disgrace of publicly renouncing the royal customs that Thomas had accepted at Clarendon. Therefore they urged the exiles to make peace without any mention of the customs, for by granting them peace the king would have implicitly conceded their abolition. But the archbishop's party insisted that the abolition of the customs be explicit, declaring that 'silence implies consent.' Besides, they urgently demanded that the goods that had been confiscated by the king during the exile be restored to them. When the cardinals reported back to King Henry II, he was furious at their lack of progress, and said that he hoped he would never set eyes on a cardinal again.[17]

After the collapse of these efforts, both sides again sent envoys to the curia. In May 1168 Pope Alexander, hoping to speed up efforts towards peace, announced that Thomas's legation would come into effect again on 5 March 1169. A new mission was sent, this time consisting of three French priors,

Thomas Becket departing from the two kings at Montmirail, miniature from the Becket Leaves, *c.* 1220–40.

and their efforts succeeded in bringing the king and the archbishop together at Montmirail near the frontier of Maine on
6 January 1169.[18] The exiles arrived at the conclusion of an
important peace summit between King Henry and King Louis.
There Henry II had proposed dividing his dominions among
his sons. The eldest, Henry, was to receive his father's inheritance of England, Normandy and Anjou; Richard (the future
Lionheart) was to receive his mother's inheritance of Aquitaine,
and was betrothed to Louis's daughter Alice; the third son,
Geoffrey, was to receive Brittany as a vassal of his brother Henry.
Henry II, Henry the Younger and Richard all paid homage to
King Louis for their lands in France. In return, Louis committed to intervene with Henry's vassals in Poitou and Brittany
who had been rebelling against him with the support of the
French king. The final part of the bargain was that Louis would
intervene with Thomas to bring about peace.

The business was conducted through mediators. King Henry
indicated that he intended to go on crusade, but that he needed
first to make peace with his archbishop. All he required from
Thomas, he said, was that he be given due honour in the presence of the French king, if only verbally. The mediators reported
back to Thomas and advised him to submit himself entirely to
the compassion and will of the king and he would find peace.
Thomas told them that he would do all this, but added the pro-
viso, 'saving God's honour'. This, of course, was an echo of his
qualified acceptance of the king's customs, 'saving our order',
back in 1163 at the Council of Westminster. The mediators
pressed Thomas to drop his qualification, impressing on him how
it would infuriate the king. Herbert says that Thomas was eventually urged, drawn, pushed and pulled so much that he seemed
persuaded. But Herbert himself managed to whisper in his master's ear, 'Lord, see that you tread carefully,' reminding him of
the sorrow caused by his concession to the king's customs at

Clarendon. Brought before the two kings, the archbishop prostrated himself at King Henry's feet, and the king immediately
took hold of him and raised him up. Then Thomas made a
humble speech in which he reproached himself for bringing great
disturbance to the Church through his own faults. And he concluded by saying, 'Therefore my lord, regarding the entire case
between you and me, I now submit myself to your mercy and
judgement in the presence of our lord king of France, and the
bishops and nobles and others present here.' But Thomas had
not quite finished. To the surprise of the king, the mediators and,
Herbert says, even his own men, he added, 'saving God's honour'.

King Henry responded with predictable fury, calling Thomas
proud, arrogant, ungrateful and treacherous. But this time King
Louis too was seen to turn against Thomas. 'Lord archbishop,'
he asked, 'do you want to be more than a saint?' When Thomas
tried to justify himself, the mediators hurried him away and they,
along with all the secular and ecclesiastical potentates, English
and French, Norman, Breton and Poitevin, and the religious
orders present, pressed him to drop that phrase, 'saving God's
honour'. Herbert describes Thomas among this crowd standing
as a sacrificial victim, surrounded by executioners, armed not
with steel but with words. But he could not be moved, and when
they all departed from him, 'the athlete of the Almighty remained
alone in the battlefield, alone in the hall of the wrestling-
school.'[19] As the exiles made their way back to Sens in the com-
pany of the king of France, King Louis shunned them, and even
some of Thomas's own party rebuked him. Yet after three days'
journey Thomas was unexpectedly summoned to Louis's presence. There, to his astonishment, the king burst out in tearful
confession, begging the archbishop to forgive him. For he said, he
had just discovered that King Henry had reneged on the agreement the two kings had made by taking vengeance on the French
king's allies. 'Truly, my lord of Canterbury, you alone could see,'

he said. 'We were all blind, we who against God advised you in your cause, or rather God's, to yield God's honour at the command of a man.'[20]

Companions in Battle

At the height of the dispute Herbert of Bosham wrote to a friend that Thomas was fighting a great struggle, 'against the world, on the stage of the world, as a spectacle for men and for angels'.[21] And this characterization of Thomas as fighting a lonely but righteous battle gained considerable strength when regarded from the perspective of his murder and posthumous glory. Now what had once seemed intransigence appeared as a perceptive recognition of reality: 'Truly, my lord of Canterbury, you alone could see.' This also shed a new light on Thomas's own character and motives, with stubbornness transformed into principle, a refusal to follow advice revealed as a selfless pursuit of truth and justice. But whichever way we choose to interpret it, a pattern of isolation – or at least aloofness – appears to run through his life. We can speculate that this was a response to moving in increasingly elevated social environments, where he needed to observe others carefully and retain his own counsel. And perhaps Thomas's close personal relationships are not as evident to us because he was not an accomplished letter-writer like John of Salisbury or others known to have cultivated friendship networks. But we have to conclude that there are few signs of Thomas maintaining close personal relationships with people on the same level, except with King Henry if we accept the testimony of his biographers. There were, though, many people who admired Thomas, well before he was hailed as a saint and even as others were abandoning him. Thomas had a loyal group of followers who saw themselves as comrades in his struggle against the world.

Herbert says that just as King David in the Bible surrounded himself with a band of mighty warriors so Thomas had his own band of warriors, armed not with swords but with morals, erudition, knowledge and good advice. And just as the Second Book of Samuel listed David's warriors,[22] so Herbert includes in his Life of Thomas a catalogue of these learned men, whom he calls the *eruditi*. The first of the *eruditi*, he says, was Thomas himself, 'more learned than all'. Next he lists Lombard of Piacenza, who taught canon law to his master in exile, and later became a cardinal and finally archbishop of Benevento. After him was John of Salisbury, 'abundant in both wisdom and knowledge', who remained steadfast with Thomas to the end, and was eventually promoted to the bishopric of Chartres. Herbert appreciated not only learning but morals and loyalty, and so he mentions Gunter of Winchester, 'a simple and upright man, fearful and without complaint', whose life more than compensated for what he lacked in learning. He also includes Thomas's cross-bearer Alexander Llewelyn. Described as 'well educated in letters, joyful in words, and abundant in joyful words', he served his lord faithfully always and everywhere, in word and deed. These men, Herbert suggests, would meet in council with the archbishop at least once a day, discussing the matters of the day, planning and providing mutual encouragement. We can see them drafting letters on the archbishop's behalf, and advising Thomas how to act on the basis of biblical and Church tradition.

Though Herbert lists himself as the last of the *eruditi*, he was unquestionably the most learned and the most devoted of Thomas's circle. In fact, he was one of the most remarkable intellectual figures of the twelfth century. Herbert studied and later taught theology and biblical exegesis at the schools of Paris, and he was Thomas's 'master of the holy page', assisting him in biblical analysis, and in relating his own struggle to past champions of the Church. Herbert wrote a number of commentaries on the Bible, one of which, on the Psalms, was only discovered in the mid-twentieth century. This discovery revealed that Herbert had consulted with Jewish scholars in investigating the literal sense of the Bible, and that he apparently had a better grasp of Hebrew than any other Western Christian contemporary known to us. Herbert had a brilliant and original mind, and his musings sometimes stray into unexpected territory. For example, he wrote of being disturbed by doubts about Christian doctrine, and wondered if the Jews were right in saying that the Lord had not yet been incarnated.[23] But Herbert was not just an intellectual. He was a man of action on whose efforts the archbishop depended. He was also a flamboyant character who drew attention to himself by his boldness in speaking to the powerful. William fitz Stephen records a meeting in 1166 between Henry II and some of Thomas's clerks who came to ask for the restoration of their confiscated properties. Herbert caused uproar by lecturing the king on the wickedness of his Constitutions and then insulting his parentage by pointing out that he was not the son of a king. Herbert is usually presented as Thomas's most uncompromising supporter, so much so that the archbishop himself had to reject his more extreme advice. He stayed with Thomas throughout his exile, but to his everlasting regret he was not present for the martyrdom. He remained ever devoted to the memory of the martyr. We find him in old age complaining of how Thomas's cause had lost its champions, and that he himself had no friend in England, 'that land of forgetfulness'.[24]

Thomas depended not only on his household in exile, but on a network of supporters. The *eruditi* maintained contacts with sympathetic churchmen in France, England and the papal curia. They gathered intelligence, roused supporters to action and spread propaganda. Perhaps the most energetic figure in these activities was John of Salisbury. John came from a humble background but gained advancement through education at Paris and

Chartres in the 1130s, and in the late 1140s he joined Archbishop
Theobald's service. John was an enthusiast for classical learning,
and he has been considered one of the finest examples of 'twelfth-
century humanism'. His writings include a defence of the liberal
arts in which he describes the cathedral schools of France, and
also a memoir of his time at the papal court in Theobald's service.
His best-known work is the *Policraticus*, which was dedicated to
Thomas Becket when he was chancellor. The *Policraticus* covers
an array of subjects but is famous for John's discussion of politics.
He addresses the distinction between the prince, who upholds
the law and supports the priesthood, and the tyrant, and describes
the 'commonwealth' in terms of the human body: the king is the
head, the priests the soul, the common people the feet. When
Thomas became archbishop, John joined his household, and in
late 1163 or early 1164 he went into exile in France, perhaps to
prepare the way for Thomas's own flight, and settled at Rheims
where his friend Peter of Celle was abbot. John often appears as
a voice of restraint. When Thomas asked him to review two drafts
of a letter he was planning to send to William of Pavia, John
wrote back: 'No – I do not approve of your drafting either of the
first or of the second letter you have resolved to send to Cardinal
William. Both seem too full of suspicion and biting sarcasm. I
fear such rashness on our part may justify both him and our other
enemies.'[25] As we shall see, John also rebuked Thomas on the
evening of his murder for provoking the knights. But he could
also have harsh words for those who infringed upon ecclesiastical
liberty. He compared Gilbert Foliot to those who plotted against
King David and his priests, and he likened other prevaricators
among the English clergy to the scribes, the Pharisees and Judas.
And although John's relationship with Thomas never appears
to have had the same intimacy as Herbert's, it was John who was
the most effective agent in promoting Thomas's veneration as
a saint.[26]

The Deadlock Is Broken

On 28 February 1169 the pope announced another mission, led by Gratian, a papal notary, and Vivian, an advocate in the papal court. A few days later, on 5 March, the suspension of Thomas's powers of censure lapsed, freeing him to take fresh measures against his enemies. On Palm Sunday, 13 April, Thomas preached at Clairvaux, the Cistercian monastery founded by St Bernard, and there he excommunicated the bishops of London and Salisbury, as well as Ranulf de Broc and his brother Robert, and other invaders of Canterbury property.[27] None of this was unexpected. London and Salisbury had already appealed in advance to the pope against such sentences, and the king had the ports watched for anyone bringing in letters from the pope or the archbishop. Nonetheless, Thomas's agents managed to break through the blockade, and on Ascension Day, 29 April, a young man named Berengar pressed into the hands of the priest celebrating Mass at St Paul's, London, the letter of excommunication of Gilbert Foliot.[28] On the very same day, in France, Thomas was issuing further sentences of excommunication. In June 1169 the pope asked him to suspend all of his recent censures until the current round of diplomacy had run its course, but that he would be free to renew them at Michaelmas (29 September) if the peace efforts failed. And this is exactly what Thomas did in the autumn, renewing his sentences of the spring and adding some more. Around the same time King Henry issued new additions to the Constitutions, which announced strict punishments for anyone bringing to England letters of interdict or observing such an interdict, and for those who appealed to the pope or archbishop or tried to leave the kingdom without permission.[29]

In the face of such rising tensions, king and archbishop were brought together again on 18 November at Montmartre, just outside Paris.[30] King Henry had come to Paris to visit the shrine of

St Denis, the patron saint of France, and to meet for the first time
King Louis's son and heir Philip, who had been born in 1165 to
the king's third wife, Adela of Champagne. Herbert suggests
that he was also eager to prevent the pope from supporting the
exiles against his interests, and calculated that Thomas would
by now have regretted his earlier intransigence at Montmirail.
The two kings met, and they were later joined by Thomas and
his men at the chapel of the Holy Martyrdom, at the foot of the
hill of Montmartre. The exiles took their places inside the chapel,
the kings remained outside, and mediators went back and forth
between them. The precise details of the negotiations are not
known, but the end result was that Henry II showed himself willing to drop all demand for Thomas to acknowledge his customs.
But neither side gave these terms clear expression, agreeing that
to do so would only disrupt the peace, nor was there any mention
of the phrase 'saving God's honour' on the archbishop's part.
All the king said was that Thomas should return to his church
as archbishop, and neither should usurp what belonged to the
other. Thomas was still concerned about recompense for his
men who had been dispossessed by the king during the exile, but
at King Louis's intervention he agreed to defer discussion of
this matter.

Now it seemed to all present that the long-awaited peace
was at hand, but there was one more obstacle to overcome. As
we have seen in the negotiations over the previous years, peace-
making was an elaborate business, involving clear and recogniz-
able steps: the pope announced a mission, the envoys would
often meet with the parties involved separately to discuss terms
before bringing them together for a choreographed conference.
But how might peace be concluded? How could it be declared
publicly that the protagonists in a dispute were in harmony and
that their followers ought to behave accordingly? One way to
do so was to bestow the kiss of peace.[31] This was not merely a

personal greeting, but an important public ritual. The problem in this case was that King Henry had at an earlier time made a vow in anger never to admit Thomas to the kiss of peace. So when Thomas sent word through his mediators that he should have an outward guarantee that peace had been re-established and favour restored, the king excused himself on the grounds of his oath, while insisting that he harboured no anger or resentment to his archbishop. When this was reported to Thomas, he answered categorically that he would not make peace with the king without the kiss of peace, and so the conference broke up, the king cursing the archbishop as he departed.

The last year of Thomas's life began then with peace seemingly as far away as ever. Thomas reimposed the sentences of the previous year and in January 1170 the pope launched yet another mission, comprised of the archbishop of Rouen, the bishop of Nevers and Cardinal William of Pavia. But whereas Cardinal William had once been seen by Becket's party as especially hostile to his cause, by now they were on much friendlier terms. Also, this most recent papal mission had a new force behind it: the legates had been instructed to threaten King Henry with interdict on his lands should he fail to agree peace with Thomas. It was not, however, these moves that brought peace. Rather, it was prompted by the action of the king.

From childhood Henry Plantagenet had been made aware of the injustice suffered by his mother, and by extension himself. Matilda had, in this telling, been deprived of her rightful inheritance, the throne of England, and Henry had spent his youth fighting for that inheritance. Disputed successions had been the norm in England since William duke of Normandy had taken the throne from King Harold by force in 1066. William II was challenged by his brother Robert Curthose, who also claimed the throne from King Henry I. But Henry II did not have to look far to find a much more smooth history of succession. The Capetian kings of France, as well as being blessed with male children, had a practice of crowning the heir to the throne during the elder king's life. Henry II's son, also called Henry, was now fifteen years old, and there had long been plans to have him crowned. Coronation was a solemn ceremony involving the anointing of the king with oil, deliberately echoing the consecration of kings in the Old Testament. Just as a priest, bishop or archbishop was changed by his consecration, so a king was set apart, his subjects warned not to put forth their hand against the Lord's anointed (1 Samuel 24:6). But the crowning of a king was the prerogative of the archbishop of Canterbury, and only in very strictly necessary circumstances could this be given to someone else. In 1161 during the vacancy that followed Archbishop Theobald's death, Henry had secured papal licence to have his son crowned at the hands of the archbishop of York, but more recently the pope had expressly prohibited the English prelates from crowning the Young Henry.[32] It is unclear whether these letters had reached the English bishops before the coronation, but none of them could have had any doubts as to how serious a violation of the privileges of the church of Canterbury this would be. Nonetheless, in March 1170 King Henry II returned to England for the first time in four years, and in his presence on 14 June at Westminster Abbey Henry the Younger was crowned king by Archbishop Roger of York, with the participation of the bishops of London, Salisbury, Durham and Rochester, and others from Wales and Normandy.[33]

For such a solemn ceremony to be carried out in the province of Canterbury, in defiance of the archbishop of Canterbury, assisted by two excommunicate bishops, in the face of a threat of interdict, and against the explicit prohibition of the pope, was a shocking transgression. Looking back on this 'profane consecration', Herbert of Bosham could identify a dire series of consequences. This outrage, he believed, had led not only to the murder of the archbishop but to the premature death of the

Coronation of Henry the Young King, miniature from the Becket
Leaves, *c.* 1220–40.

Young Henry and his brother Geoffrey, both of whom prede-
ceased their father.[34] There were more immediate consequences
too. Thomas wrote to the pope, asking him to impose censures
on the bishops involved in the coronation. William 'of the
White Hands', archbishop of Sens and papal legate in France,
called for the imposition of an interdict on King Henry's continental lands. Pope Alexander wrote to Henry II urging him to
restore peace to his archbishop, and instructed that an interdict
be imposed on the kingdom of England should Henry defy the
pope's admonitions.[35] There was little option for the king but
to agree to peace with his archbishop. Indeed fitz Stephen claims
that one of the king's men said to him, 'Why do you persist in
keeping the archbishop abroad? It would be better to have him
in England than out of it.'[36]

On 22 July, at the end of a conference with King Louis,
Henry and Thomas met on horseback near Fréteval. Thomas
described their meeting in a letter to the pope, reporting that

When he saw us approaching in the distance, leaving
the crowd milling around him, he advanced closer, and,
with his head uncovered he anticipated our salutation,
exultantly pouring forth words of greeting, and after
saying a few words in the presence of ourselves and the
lord of Sens, he turned aside, and to the amazement of
everyone, led us apart and spoke for a long time with
such familiarity that it seemed there had never been any
discord between us.

They avoided all discussion of the customs, though Thomas did
complain to the king of the coronation, and the king attempted
to defend it. Then Thomas dismounted and knelt at the king's
feet, and when he was about to remount, the king held Thomas's
stirrup for him, saying tearfully, 'Let us restore the old affection
between us, and each show what favour he can to the other; and
let us forthwith forget the enmity that has gone before; but I ask
you to show me respect in the presence of those who are watch-
ing from afar.' A little later they made the final agreement. The
archbishop of Sens asked on their behalf that the king restore
the archbishop and his men to his favour, and that he grant them
peace and security to return to Canterbury and their possessions,
and to correct the grievance caused by the Young King's coronation, and in return they promised the king affection, honour
and service. This time the archbishop did not ask for a kiss of
peace nor was it offered.[37]

Both Henry and Thomas must have realized that it was impossible to turn back the clock to a time of affection and favour.
Too many people had become entangled in the dispute in the
intervening years. There were many who would rejoice at
Thomas's restitution. These included his own family and friends
who had been persecuted and expelled from the kingdom, the
monks of Canterbury who would finally have their pastor restored

to them, and more broadly those people of the diocese of Canterbury who looked to their archbishop for spiritual guidance and material support. Many too within the hierarchy of the Church in England and beyond would be relieved that the prolonged disruption caused by the schism between king and archbishop seemed at last to have been put to rest. But Thomas's restoration necessitated the dispossession of those to whom the lands and properties of the see of Canterbury had been committed, and those clerks who had been presented to vacant churches during the exile. Thomas's return also stifled the ambitions of Roger of York and Gilbert of London, who had shown themselves willing to take the reins of the English Church at the king's invitation. Then there was the coronation of the Young King. To let the slight on Canterbury go unpunished would create a dreadful precedent, but to take action would bring Thomas into conflict with the bishops, the king and his son. And above all there remained the resentments that had been fed by years of slights and offences on all sides.

A few weeks after the meeting at Fréteval Thomas sent Herbert of Bosham and John of Salisbury to the king at Domfront to ask about the restoration of properties, but finding him seriously ill with fever, they made little progress. When the king had recovered and the archbishop himself paid him a visit, he was shown a stern countenance, and told that restoration of his estates would only happen when he had returned to Canterbury. A few days later they met again, and this time Henry promised that he would join him at Rouen, where he would pay off the archbishop's creditors and either accompany him in person to England or ask Archbishop Rotrou of Rouen to do so.[38] On 15 October King Henry sent instructions to his son:

> Be it known to you that Thomas, archbishop of
> Canterbury, has made peace with me according to my

will. I therefore command that he and all his men shall
have peace. You are to ensure that the archbishop and all
his men, who left England for his sake, shall enjoy their
possessions in peace and honour, as they held them three
months before the archbishop withdrew from England.[39]

Yet even as Thomas prepared to return to England, he began to
hear disturbing news from his clerks Herbert and John, whom
he had sent ahead to prepare the way. They reported that the
archbishop's men had been expelled by royal officials when they
sought to take possession of their estates, and that the king had
recruited York, London and Salisbury to elect bishops to vacant
sees without consulting Thomas:

> Again and again, my lord, we impress on your memory,
> that you should not hurry into England unless you are
> able to secure the unadulterated grace of the lord king.
> For there is no man in England, even among those you
> trust, who does not despair entirely of the peace.[40]

In mid-November Thomas left Sens for the last time, equipped
by French nobles with clothes, horses and an escort, and arrived
at Rouen for his rendezvous with King Henry. But there instead
he found John of Oxford, the man whom Thomas had excommunicated in 1166 for his dealings with the schismatic Frederick
Barbarossa, with a message from the king: he could not accompany him to England because he had information about a French
offensive in the Auvergne. Nor had the archbishop of Rouen
received any instructions to accompany Thomas across the
Channel, and the king had not even provided money for the
expedition or to pay his debtors – Thomas was obliged to take
a gift of £300 from Rotrou's own money. A few days later Thomas
came with his escort, John of Oxford, to the port of Wissant in

Thomas Becket warned as he embarks for England, miniature from the
Becket Leaves, c. 1220–40.

Flanders. There he met the dean of Boulogne, who warned him
of reports from England that his enemies – presumably Ranulf
de Broc and his men – were lying in wait, preparing to seize and
kill him or put him in chains. Nonetheless, Thomas determined
to cross the Channel, and he set sail on 1 December.[41]

But before he set sail, he had a last piece of business to deal
with. In November a messenger had arrived from the pope with
letters that had been written and dispatched some months before
when Alexander had heard some especially damaging reports
about the coronation. Among these were letters ordering the
suspension from office of Archbishop Roger of York and all of
those who officiated in the coronation back in July (with the
exception of the bishop of Exeter) and the renewal of the sentences of excommunication against Bishops Gilbert of London
and Jocelin of Salisbury. Just before his own passage to England,
Thomas sent these letters ahead with a boy named Osbern, who
found York, London and Salisbury at Dover waiting to cross the

Channel to see the king. As William fitz Stephen writes, when the bishops read the 'thundering judgement', their faces were pushed to the ground.[42]

SIX

Murder

After his death, many seemingly prophetic anecdotes were told of Thomas's last days and weeks. In his final meeting with the king at Chaumont, he is said to have told Henry, 'Lord, my heart tells me that in taking my leave of you now, I will not see you again in this life.' In taking his leave of King Louis, Thomas said that he was going to England 'to play for heads', and likewise he told the bishop of Paris, 'I am going into England to die.'[1] When Thomas reached the Flemish coast some of his men pointed to the good sailing conditions and said, 'Why do you not get into the ship? Will we be like Moses, who saw the promised land but did not enter it?' 'Why rush?', replied Thomas. 'Within forty days from your entry into the land you will wish to be in any other land than in England.'[2] It is easy to dismiss these as retrospective fabrications, but similar words were also used at the time. John of Salisbury wrote to a friend in France of the atmosphere of intrigue, persecution and hatred that he found on his return to Canterbury. Here, he said, 'we await God's salvation in great danger.'[3] 'Fate is drawing me, unhappy wretch that I am, to that afflicted church,' wrote Thomas in his last surviving letter to King Henry.

> I shall return to her, perhaps to die, to prevent her destruction, unless your piety deigns swiftly to offer us some other comfort. But whether we live or die, we are

and will always be yours in the Lord; and whatever happens
to us and ours, may God bless you and your children.[4]

Thomas and those around him knew that his return to Canterbury
might be dangerous, but they could not have expected things
to turn out quite as they did. The murder of the archbishop of
Canterbury in his own cathedral was an event that shocked
even those who had come to fear the worst. England was one
of the safest and most ordered places in Europe, and the age of
the martyrs appeared to be long gone. It is only by appreciating
the brutality and the sacrilege of the act, and the shock that it
provoked, that we can appreciate the outpouring of grief that
followed. In the light of the murder, everything seemed different. As the monks stripped the body for burial, they discovered
the monastic habit and hairshirt, and 'all ran up to view – clad
in sackcloth – him whom as chancellor they had seen clothed in
purple and satin'.[5] Now people began to speak of what William
fitz Stephen called 'this double martyrdom, the voluntary one of
his life and the violent one of his death', and how the two formed
a unity. But as well as transforming Thomas's reputation, the murder would have immediate consequences for others: for the
monks of Canterbury, the English bishops and above all for
the king.

Return to Canterbury

Expecting ambushes, Thomas's party diverted from the port of
Dover where they would have been expected to land, and instead
put in at Sandwich, a fief of the church of Canterbury.[6] As the
ship came into sight, distinguished by the archbishop's cross
towering above it, a crowd of poor people ran to meet it, throwing themselves on the ground, weeping for joy and crying out,
'Blessed is he who comes in the name of the Lord, father of

orphans and judge of widows!' It was not long, however, before
they were met by a less friendly group, agents of the king who
angrily demanded an explanation of his suspension and excommunication of the king's bishops, accusing him of disturbing the
peace of the Church and the kingdom. Thomas answered that
he had no wish to deprive the Young King of his crown, but that
the coronation had been done against the dignity of Canterbury
and that justice must be done. The next day Thomas made the
10-kilometre (6 mi.) journey from the seashore to Canterbury,
and there the archbishop entered his cathedral for the first time
in over six years. The priests and their parishioners came out of
the city in procession to meet him, accompanied by throngs of
ordinary people, young and old, calling for his blessing. Had you
seen it, writes Herbert of Bosham, you would have thought that
Christ was for a second time approaching his Passion, and that
He who had once died at Jerusalem to save the whole world had
come again to die at Canterbury for the English Church. The
crowds were such that Thomas could hardly reach his own
church, but finally, to the sounds of bells ringing, organs playing
and hymns being sung, he was received by his community of
monks. But again, acclaim was soon followed by threat. The
king's agents returned, seeking answers to the questions they
had addressed to him the day before, and they were joined by
clerks of the censured bishops, who demanded their absolution.
Thomas answered that he would submit their cases to judgement by the pope if the prelates would take an oath to abide by
such a judgement. These men departed in indignation, and Ranulf
de Broc is reported to have gone out of his way to insult the
archbishop.[7]

   After a few days at Canterbury, Thomas set out for Winchester,
intending to visit the Young King there, and bringing with him
three valuable warhorses as a gift. He passed through London
on the way, and as he approached Southwark on the south bank

Thomas Becket landing at Sandwich and blessing the water, miniature
from the Becket Leaves, *c.* 1220–40.

of the Thames, great crowds of clergy and people came out to
meet him, among them a large group of scholars and clerks. But
when the archbishop reached London he was met by envoys of
the Young King, who told him that he was not welcome at his
court, and that he should instead return to his church. The archbishop's party turned around and set off for Canterbury, where
he would remain for the last weeks of his life. There he heard
further disturbing news, this time of outrages against his men
and his property at the hands of the de Broc family. They had
set guards along the roads leading out of Canterbury to make
sure that Thomas did not leave. They had seized a transport ship
bringing wine to the archbishop and had used violence and
imprisonment against the sailors. They had hunted in his park
and stolen his hunting-dogs. And one of them had intercepted
a delivery of provisions on horseback and had cut off the horse's
tail as an insult to the archbishop. Through all this, say his biographers, Thomas remained determined, seeing these as signs of

his impending martyrdom. William of Canterbury says that when the archbishop was warned of danger, he only touched his neck and said, 'Here, here the boys will find me.' According to fitz Stephen, Thomas began to devote himself increasingly to almsgiving, prayer and care of his soul. In these days he would often hint at his death, saying that the dispute could only be resolved through bloodshed, and that he was prepared to persist in the Church's cause to the end.[8]

On Christmas Day Thomas celebrated Mass in the cathedral and delivered a sermon. In tears, he reminded the congregation that they already had one martyr, Aelfheah, killed by Danes in 1012 when he refused to pay tribute, and predicted that they would soon have another. Herbert says that as the congregation called out to him, 'Father, why do you desert us so soon?', Thomas now no longer weeping, but instead furious and bold, inveighed against those who hated peace. Unwilling to keep the sword sheathed, he says, Thomas wielded it boldly and confidently and struck with anathema many of the courtiers closest to the king, and particularly Ranulf and Robert de Broc. The next day, the feast of St Stephen, the first Christian martyr, Thomas called Herbert into his presence and informed him that he was sending him on business to King Louis, to the archbishop of Sens and to other friends in France, to inform them of the failure of the peace. Herbert, distraught, complained that 'I who was a companion in your struggle will not be a companion in your glory.' Thomas reassured him that he would always share in his glory, but conceded, 'what you say and lament is true: you will never see me again in the flesh.'[9]

Herbert, along with his other biographers, believed that Thomas willingly embraced martyrdom for the cause of God and the Church. This is also what many multitudes came to believe in the aftermath of his murder, and this would become the official view of the Church as expressed in the papal bull of canonization issued on 21 February 1173. Some, however, have come to a similar but more critical conclusion about Thomas's last days: that Thomas deliberately brought a violent death upon himself, seeing it as the surest way to victory. In T. S. Eliot's play *Murder in the Cathedral* this is a course that Thomas considered and rejected, the embrace of martyrdom for the glory that it would bring: 'The last temptation is the greatest treason: To do the right deed for the wrong reason.'[10] But for all the signs of danger, and recorded prophesies of his death, other indications suggest that Thomas was acting in a way incongruous with one prepared to die. His sending of Herbert to rouse their allies in France is one such move, and Herbert himself tells us that Thomas explained that he was sending him away because 'the king sees you as more troublesome than others in the cause of the Church.'[11] Similarly, Thomas's letters in December 1170 show him continuing to conduct routine business. Though fully conscious of the rising tensions, Thomas's actions in these final weeks and days do not necessarily suggest that he saw his death as imminent, or that he brought it on himself. But already matters that Thomas himself had set in train were taking on a life of their own.

The newly excommunicated and suspended English prelates had crossed to France and a few days before Christmas they were received by the king at Bur-le-Roi in Normandy. One of the most widely attested characteristics of Henry II was his furious anger. In 1166 an anonymous correspondent described to Thomas Henry's reaction when someone in his presence had praised the king of Scotland with whom he was in dispute at the time:

Consequently, the king, alarmed with his usual rage, tore his hat from his head, undid his belt, hurled his cloak and the clothes he was wearing far away from him, tore the

silken covering from the bed with his own hand, and
began to eat the straw on the floor, as if he was sitting
in a ditch.[12]

Anger could be useful for a king – it could be deployed stra-
tegically to intimidate and to signal displeasure. But here, in
Bur-le-Roi, in late December, hearing the prelates' grievances
against Thomas, King Henry's temper erupted in a way that had
consequences that he could not have imagined. If there is an
expression commonly associated with Thomas's murder it is the
words attributed to King Henry: 'Who will rid me of this turbulent
priest?', or perhaps, 'Who will rid me of this *troublesome* priest?'[13]
In fact, there is no contemporary record of such words, and those
reported by Thomas's medieval biographers are more expressive
and revealing. According to Guernes, when the king saw the
letters of censure he was very angry, and struck his hands together.
He went away into his room white with fury, saying that he had
raised evil men, cared for them and gave them his bread, but not
one of them would take any share in his grief. His men turned to
each other, alarmed at the king's distress but unclear as to its
cause. But then the king spoke to them:

> A man who has eaten my bread, who came to my court
> poor, and I have raised him high – now he draws up his
> heel to kick me in the teeth! He has shamed my kin,
> shamed my realm; the grief goes to my heart, and no
> one has avenged me!

Other accounts share the same allusion to the ingratitude of
one who had been raised up from nothing. According to William
of Canterbury, Henry denounced Thomas as 'a man who first
burst into my court with a knapsack and a limping mule' and
now raises up his heel, trying to seize the throne for himself.[14]

In response to the king's angry words the whole court began to issue fierce threats against the archbishop. Some of them started to bind themselves together by oath to swiftly avenge the king's shame. The four men inspired to take vengeance were Reginald fitz Urse, Hugh de Morville, William de Tracy and Richard Brito. They are traditionally referred to as 'knights', but this does not quite capture the reality of their position as young but quite substantial barons. Recent investigations have drawn attention to some interesting aspects of their background.[15] First, many of the murderers had connections to Thomas when he was chancellor. For example, fitz Urse, who is often presented as the leader of the group, had apparently been introduced to the royal court by Thomas himself. Also, although the three most distinguished of the knights – fitz Urse, Morville and Tracy – all held extensive lands, they were on the fringes rather than at the centre of King Henry's court. They came from families that had been loyal to King Stephen during the 'Anarchy', and they may have been all the more anxious to prove themselves to King Henry. The four slipped away from court and made a quick passage across the sea to Kent – Thomas's biographers claim that this was divine providence, urging on Thomas's sacrifice. The day after his initial outburst, King Henry is said to have raged against Thomas again in the presence of his magnates, and at that meeting some of his older barons told the king that there was no other way to deal with such a man but through violence. But when the king heard that the four 'knights' had left his court, he sent envoys after them, perhaps to recall them. It was too late. On 28 December the knights had arrived at the seat of the de Broc family, Saltwood Castle, 13 kilometres (8 mi.) from Canterbury.

Canterbury, 29 December 1170

There are few events in medieval history as well attested as the murder of Thomas Becket in Canterbury Cathedral on 29 December 1170.[16] Five of those who wrote about it were present in the cathedral: the clerks William fitz Stephen and John of Salisbury, the monks Benedict and William, as well as Edward Grim, a clerk from Cambridge. Edward had not met Thomas before December 1170, but was an admirer of his and had visited Canterbury to meet him. He would write one of the earliest and fullest descriptions of the murder and would also gain a lasting place in the iconography of the murder, thanks to his bravery before the knights' swords. Many other contemporaries wrote their own accounts, based on the witness of others, notably Herbert of Bosham who provides copious original detail and interpretation. Everything happened very quickly, the cathedral was dimly lit, memories can be defective and witnesses can be influenced by the accounts of others. But yet there is a great degree of consistency across the accounts, and we can be confident in the broad shape of what happened. It is just as important to realize, though, that when people wrote down what they had witnessed or heard from others, they were interested in both recounting what had happened and in explaining what it meant. It was not only a brutal murder but a martyrdom – a willing death on behalf of the Church. Therefore, the accounts of Thomas's death are permeated with imagery familiar from accounts of Christ's Passion and those of the early Christian martyrs. At the same time, these writers considered the murder as the culmination or fulfilment of Thomas's whole life: Herbert called it 'the consummation'. This meant that, just as they retrospectively imbued elements of Thomas's early years, advancement and conflict with the king with forebodings of his end, so they used his last moments to reflect on his life as a whole. Here I will follow the accounts, and in particular that of Edward Grim,[17] pausing occasionally, like the contemporary writers themselves, to reflect on what was happening.

The knights arrived at Canterbury around three o'clock in the afternoon. They had come from Saltwood Castle, accompanied by other knights whom they had called out from royal garrisons in Kent and along the way. The larger force remained outside when the four knights, with some accomplices, entered the archbishop's palace. Thomas had just finished dining and had withdrawn to a chamber to transact some business with his household when it was announced to him that four men had come to speak to him on behalf of the king. When they were led in, they gave the archbishop no greeting, and did not address a word to him. He too remained silent for a time, carefully examining each face in turn, until finally he greeted them in peace. To this, the knights responded with curses, and sarcastically called on God to help the archbishop. Then Reginald fitz Urse, who appeared to be their leader, said, 'We have something to say to you on the king's orders; if you wish us to say it before all, speak.' Thomas, knowing what they were going to say, insisted that they say it in public, so fitz Urse laid out the complaints against him. He recalled how peace had been made, and the archbishop had been restored to his see, but he had gone on to violate the peace by issuing anathemas against the participants in the coronation. It is clear from this act, said fitz Urse, that Thomas wanted to deprive the Young Henry of his crown. 'If you deign to respond to these charges in the presence of the king', concluded fitz Urse, 'say so. That is why we have been sent.'[18] If we believe this account, the purpose of the knights' mission is clear. They had not come to Canterbury to murder the archbishop. Rather, they demanded that he go with them to give an account of his actions before the king. In other words, their purpose was to arrest Thomas. The problem, as we will soon see,

Martyrdom of Thomas Becket, c. 1260, fresco (now detached), Palazzo dei Trecento, Treviso.

is that such limited plans could easily tip over into violence, when angry and fully armed knights came into contact with Thomas's intransigence.

Thomas in reply said that he had no wish to take the crown away from the king's son and was prepared to make amends to him should he have offended in any way, but he was prohibited from travelling outside of Canterbury. Nor, he insisted, had he himself suspended the bishops – the sentence against them came from the pope. The knights, refusing to accept this, demanded that Thomas and his men leave the kingdom and the king's dominions, claiming that this was an order from the king himself, 'For neither you nor any of your men will have peace from this day on, you who violated the peace.' 'Cease your threats and quiet your brawling,' replied Thomas. 'I trust in the King of heaven Who suffered for His people on the cross. From this day forth no-one will see the sea between me and my church. I did not come back to flee. He who seeks me will find me here.' When the knights again rebuked him for sentencing the bishops, rather than bowing to royal majesty, Thomas shot back that he would spare no one who presumed to violate the laws of the Church.

Struck by these words the knights sprang to their feet, and coming near said to him, 'We warn you that you have spoken in danger to your head.' 'Have you come to kill me then?', said Thomas.

> I have committed my cause to the Judge of all, so I am
> not moved by threats, nor are your swords more ready
> to strike than my soul is ready for martyrdom. Look all
> you like for one who will run away; for you will find me
> foot to foot in the battle of the Lord.

The knights stormed out amid insults and confusion, not before commanding Thomas's clerks and monks in the king's name to seize and guard him so that he would not escape the king's justice by flight. As they left, Thomas followed them to the door and called out, 'Here, here you will find me,' putting his hand on his neck.[19] One account has John of Salisbury rebuking the archbishop for his provocative response to the knights and urging him to be more conciliatory.[20]

One might wonder why Edward Grim (and other biographers too) devote so much attention to this back-and-forth between Thomas and his killers. Certainly it illustrates the intentions of the knights, the issues at dispute between them and the archbishop, and also the dangerously heated atmosphere that prevailed. But another reason is that this presentation of events shows Thomas not only as the victim of murder, but as a martyr of the Church. The martyrs were the earliest Christian saints. They were those men and women who stood steadfast in their faith even in the face of the most horrific persecution under the rule of the pagan Roman emperors from Nero to Diocletian. The popular image of the early Christian martyrs is of their being thrown to the lions in the Roman amphitheatre or facing gladiators or terrible tortures, and the early accounts of the martyrs do indeed describe such tortures and their endurance. But suffering was not the sole meaning of martyrdom. And so, when the early Christians wrote of the martyrs' last moments, they usually did not focus as much on the tortures and violent death of the martyr as they did on his or her steadfast insistence on following Christ. The central drama is not so much the martyr being torn apart by wild animals as it is their refusal to sacrifice to Roman gods, their insistence that they will not submit to threats or persuasion, often simply the repeated statement, 'I am a Christian.' In the same way Thomas's refusal to submit to the demands of the knights is a manifestation of his status as a martyr, just as much as is his later bowing of his head to the swords.[21]

The knights had left the archbishop's chamber not to retreat but to rearm. Thomas meanwhile returned to where he had been sitting and consoled his men and told them not to be afraid. And it seemed to those present, adds Edward in a phrase often used of the early martyrs, that the archbishop was as undaunted as if they had come to invite him to a wedding. But soon his men would have further cause for fear. The knights, now dressed in full armour, carrying swords, hatchets and axes, tried to re-enter the archbishop's palace, but found that the doors had been locked. When their hammering at the doors went unanswered, they turned aside through an orchard where they found a place of entrance to the palace only obstructed by a wooden barrier. This they hacked at and split open, making a dreadful uproar and terrifying the archbishop's servants and clerks, scattering some of them, Edward writes, 'as sheep before wolves'. Those who remained with Thomas urged him to find a place of greater safety, and there was an obvious place nearby. The cathedral church of Canterbury provided sanctuary, in the sense of a most sacred space, but also a place of refuge. Thomas's initial reaction, we are told, was to refuse to flee to the church, preferring to fall to the swords than to see God's law scorned. Equally, he who had for a long time burned with love of martyrdom, and now seemed to have attained it, feared lest his hope of this outcome be dashed should he flee to the church. The monks persisted, trying to persuade him that it was not right for him to be absent from the evening office of vespers, which were then being sung in the church. But when he could be moved neither by argument nor pleas, the monks seized him and dragged, pushed and pulled him, protesting and resisting all the time, into the sanctuary of the church.[22]

Murder in the Cathedral

Those within the church broke off singing vespers when they heard the commotion, and ran up to the archbishop, giving thanks that the man they had heard was dead was alive and un-harmed. They bolted the door, so as to prevent the knights from entering, but Thomas rebuked them, saying, 'It is not right to turn the house of prayer, the church of Christ, into a fortress.' And demanding that they unbar the door, he added, 'We will triumph over the enemy not by fighting but by suffering, for we have come to suffer, not to resist.' Thomas's enemies had been following with swift strides, and soon there appeared before the monks the four knights, accompanied by a certain sub-deacon, Hugh of Horsea, nicknamed Mauclerk, or 'evil clerk'. The spectacle must have been terrifying. In the twilight of a late December evening, in the cathedral lit only by candles, the four knights were dressed from head to toe in armour, their helmets on and their visors down, so that only their eyes could be seen. In their hands they carried drawn swords and axes. Just the sight of them and the clatter of armour alone was, says Edward, enough to inflict terror on the onlookers.[23] Indeed fitz Stephen says that at this point all of Thomas's clerks, including John of Salisbury, ran to altars or other hiding places, except for Thomas's confessor Robert of Merton, Edward Grim and fitz Stephen himself.[24]

'Where is Thomas Becket, traitor to the king and the kingdom?', cried out the knights as they entered. As well as being an allegation of treachery, these words carried the taste of social condescension. For to call him 'Becket' – rather than his proper title, Archbishop, or Archbishop Thomas – was a pointed reminder of his roots in London as a merchant's son. Thomas gave no response, and now the knights shouted again, even more vehemently, 'Where is the archbishop?' Thomas stepped forward, and in a perfectly clear voice answered, 'Here I am, no traitor to the king, but a priest. What do you want from me?' He continued, 'See, I am ready to suffer in the name of Him who redeemed me with His blood.' At this he turned to the right, under a pillar, between the altar of the Virgin Mary and the altar of St Benedict. The knights followed him, demanding that he restore those he had excommunicated and suspended. Thomas replied that they had made no satisfaction for their transgressions, so he would not absolve them. 'Then', they declared, 'you will now die and get what you deserve.' Thomas fearlessly replied, 'I am prepared to die for my Lord so that in my blood the church may find liberty and peace, but I forbid you in the name of Almighty God to harm my men, whether clerk or lay, in any way.'[25] Fitz Stephen, more succinctly, has Thomas say to the knights, 'What do you want?', to which they replied, 'Your death.'[26]

The next moments, when an attempted arrest turned into murder, are the most critical. But unsurprisingly, considering that few remained to witness it and those themselves were caught up in the struggle, the details are disputed. Edward Grim tells us that at the archbishop's defiant words, the knights rushed at him and laid their hands on him, 'roughly manhandling and dragging him, intending to kill him outside the church, or carry him away in chains, as they later admitted'. But since he could not easily be moved from the pillar where he was standing, fitz Urse began to drag him away from the spot in a particularly fierce manner. At this, Thomas pushed him way, 'calling him a pimp', and saying, 'Do not touch me, Reginald, you who by right owe me fealty and obedience. You and your accomplices are acting like fools.' But inflamed with terrible fury, fitz Urse brandished his sword against the archbishop's head saying, 'I do not owe you fealty or obedience against fidelity to my lord king.' Thomas, seeing that his hour was at hand, and that the immortal crown of martyrdom was within his grasp, bent his head as if in prayer, joined his hands together and lifted them up, and commended his cause and that of the Church to God, St Mary and the martyr St Denis.[27]

Others tell it somewhat differently. According to fitz Stephen, one of the knights struck Thomas with the flat of his sword between the shoulders, saying, 'Fly, you are a dead man!', or in Benedict's account, 'You are our prisoner, you will come with us.' William of Canterbury, who was also present, says that fitz Urse knocked off the archbishop's cap with the point of his sword. Herbert of Bosham presents a dramatic alternative narrative of this moment. In his account, one of the knights, whom he names as William de Tracy, came up close to the archbishop and tried to seize him, at which 'the archbishop, taking him by his hauberk, shook him off with such force that he almost prostrated him on the pavement'. An anonymous writer too says that when fitz Urse laid hands on him and pressed on him with great force, Thomas shook him off and dashed him away from himself with such force that he almost knocked him on the floor, saying to him, 'Get back! You are my man and you ought not touch me.'[28] Though neither of the latter two writers witnessed the event, it is yet possible that their accounts retain a more accurate reminiscence of the event than the peaceable image presented by some other writers. For it was at this moment that one of the knights was provoked to strike the first blow.

Edward Grim says that fitz Urse, fearing that Thomas would be snatched by the people and escape alive, suddenly leapt on him and wounded him in the head, cutting off the top of the crown. He adds, 'The same blow almost cut off the arm of this witness who, as everyone fled, monks and clerks, steadfastly stood by the archbishop, and held him in his arms until his arm was struck.' Edward Grim's statement as to his own bravery is borne out by other witnesses, and thereafter Edward would regularly appear in visual depictions of the murder, standing by the archbishop and trying to block the path of the sword with his arm. Then Thomas received another blow in the head, perhaps from William de Tracy, but remained immovable. But at the third blow, writes Edward, the archbishop bent his knees and elbows, offering himself as a living sacrifice, saying in a low voice, 'For

Martyrdom of Thomas Becket, c. 1180, fresco, Church of Santa Maria, Terrassa.

the name of Jesus and the wellbeing of the Church I am prepared to embrace death.' Then, as he lay prostrate on the ground, a third knight, identified by some as Richard Brito, inflicted a blow of such power that the sword was dashed upon the pavement, and Thomas's crown was removed from his head. The next detail is the most horrifying and graphic. While the fourth knight, Hugh de Morville, warded off those arriving on the scene, a fifth, not a knight but the above-mentioned clerk who had come with them, 'Mauclerk', put his foot on Thomas's neck, and with the point of his sword, scattered his brains and blood on the pavement. 'Let us go, knights,' he called out to the others, 'this fellow will not get up again'.

Aftermath

As the knights left the church they called out their rallying cry, 'King's men, king's men!' Before leaving Canterbury for Saltwood Castle, they ran through the archbishop's palace, ransacking chests and cupboards and carrying off jewels, money and other valuables, an act that the biographers compare to the division of Christ's garments. William fitz Stephen adds that in a parallel to the Crucifixion the sun averted its eyes and veiled the day with darkness, and a great storm broke, followed by a redness in the air, as if in token of the blood recently shed. 'The sons slew their father in the womb of their mother,' he concludes, expressing the horror of a sacrilegious murder by Christians of their spiritual father in the most hallowed spot of the mother church of England. But when Thomas lay dead on the floor of Canterbury Cathedral, he was not yet a saint, and not yet that church's most precious possession. The Canterbury monks had never warmed to their non-monastic archbishop, whose extended exile had led the king to confiscate their lands. Their lukewarm support of Thomas during his struggle had drawn rebukes from his circle who accused them of living in luxury while the exiles struggled for justice.[29] Now, as the knights threatened further reprisals, it seemed as if in death he would bring ruin upon them.

One of the monks, Benedict of Peterborough, provides us with an intimate account of the aftermath of the murder and how their perception of Thomas changed. He says that when the archbishop's body was raised from the floor of the cathedral where it lay, they found an iron mallet and a hatchet underneath him. Blood lay around his head in the likeness of a crown, but his face seemed entirely free from blood, except for a thin line which descended from his right temple to his left cheek. As he lay on the pavement, some of those present daubed their eyes with his blood, others cut off parts of their clothes and dipped them in the blood, while those who had brought little vessels took away as much as they could. The remaining blood was carefully collected in a vessel and kept in the church. The monks placed the body before the High Altar, and spent the night in vigil around it. That lamentable night, says Benedict, was spent in sorrow, groans and sighs, awaiting a greater evil the next day. The next morning rumours spread that the knights were planning to return to snatch away and desecrate the archbishop's body. In fear and haste, the monks neither washed nor embalmed the body, but hurried to strip it for burial. Then, as they were taking off his outer garments to put on his pontifical vestments they discovered Thomas's monastic habit, and below that, right down to his knees, the hairshirt. 'The monks looked at each other', says Benedict, 'and were astonished at this view of hidden religion beyond what could have been believed. And with their sorrow thus multiplied, so were their tears.'[30]

There is broad agreement about what happened on the evening of 29 December 1170. But as to what it meant, that is something that immediately provoked debate, and that has remained open to question to this day. The view that Thomas had died a martyr's death soon gained wide acceptance, first locally among the ordinary people of Canterbury and its environs, and then among the clergy and nobility of England and beyond. But if he had died a martyr's death, did that mean that he had lived the life of a saint? And if so, how did this new image of the saintly Thomas accord with that of the merchant's son, the worldly chancellor and the controversial archbishop? In time, Thomas's admirers would shape a narrative of his life that presented it as a definite if not always obvious path to sanctity, one that was only fully revealed by his death and the miracles that followed. Perhaps more surprisingly, most of those who had been hostile to Thomas in life came to accept him as a saint, and some even came to appropriate his memory to their own ends.

According to William fitz Stephen, the first miracle occurred on the very same night as the murder. One of the townspeople of Canterbury who had been present in the cathedral when Thomas was killed dipped part of his shirt in the martyr's blood. This man's wife had been paralysed for many years, and when he returned home and told her what he had witnessed, she took hope in the martyr and asked to be washed with the saint's blood mixed in the water. This was done, and she was immediately cured.[31] This first recorded miracle set the tone in three ways. First, the recognition of Thomas as a saint was immediate and spontaneous. Second, its impetus came from the ordinary people of Canterbury, and though it would soon spread far more widely, both geographically and socially, Thomas remained a saint of Canterbury, and one who had genuine popular acclaim. Third, a distinctive feature of St Thomas's cult was 'the water of St Thomas'. A drop of Thomas's blood, mixed with water, came to be distributed to pilgrims in tin ampules, thereby allowing direct contact between the saint and the faithful, wherever they may be.

Popular devotion to saints was a central aspect of medieval life. In any society, certain people are singled out for special remembrance and respect after death, but medieval Christians believed that the elect could intervene in earthly affairs by appearing in visions or performing extraordinary acts of healing or vengeance. The living honoured these special departed in ritualized ways. This might be as simple as recording a name in a calendar and dedicating prayers to that saint every year on their feast day. Commonly, it involved visiting the saint's tomb and revering the saint's relics – pieces of the dead person's body or objects associated with that person. By the twelfth century, recognition of sanctity tended to involve translation – the placing of the saint's body in a new and often elaborate tomb – and canonization. Though we commonly think of sanctity as being determined by papal canonization, this in fact only became expected in Western Europe during Thomas's lifetime. Before that, the recognition of saints was often a local phenomenon and thereafter too many saints would have little more than a local reach.[32]

Saints met a need, or a variety of needs, and different societies produced different kinds of saints. The first saints were martyrs, who stood as examples to the faithful of adhesion to Christ, no matter what persecutions might be suffered. When Christianity became the official religion of the Roman Empire and began to spread rapidly, new types of saints emerged. These included ascetics, such as St Anthony, who retreated to the desert to punish his body and struggle with demons. As the institutional Church developed in Western Europe, saints were found in monasteries, nunneries and bishops' palaces, representing the ideal fulfilment of a specific type of religious life. There were virgins, hermits and child saints, some only venerated locally, others throughout the Christian world. Medieval England had its own illustrious catalogue of saints including the monk-bishop Cuthbert, the missionary Boniface, Queen Aethelthryth and King Edward the Martyr. But why was it that Thomas Becket was hailed as a saint so rapidly and so spectacularly?

Pilgrims healed at Thomas Becket's tomb, 13th century, stained glass, Canterbury Cathedral.

Popular acclaim was certainly an important factor. In recent times there had been attempts to claim Thomas's predecessor Anselm as a saint, but they faltered in part because there was simply little evidence of a popular cult. In the case of Edward the Confessor, it took insistent efforts by the monks of Westminster and by King Henry II to have him canonized in the face of broad public apathy. In contrast, enthusiasm for St Thomas was spontaneous, genuine and unstoppable. But popular acclaim was never enough. Ecclesiastical authorities were often suspicious of popular cults, especially of controversial individuals who had met a violent death. Part of this was a fear that veneration might become the focus for further disturbance, but it also reflected a certain upper-class distaste for vulgar superstition. It seems that the cult of St Thomas took some time to gain respectability. The Canterbury monk Benedict says that the very night of the murder, the archbishop appeared to him in a vision. 'Are you not dead, lord?', the monk asked him, to which Thomas replied, 'I was dead, but I rose again.' Benedict asked him why he did not show himself to the world, and Thomas answered, 'I carry a light, but it cannot appear because a cloud is in the way.' This, the monk explained, was the 'cloud of persecution' that persisted until after Easter 1171. Before that, people in Canterbury and beyond felt the miraculous power of the martyr, but it was not yet considered safe to broadcast it, on account of fear of the archbishop's enemies. But at Easter the monks opened the crypt where Thomas was buried to the public. They also took the precaution of surrounding the tomb with a strong wall, with openings for the pilgrims to touch the body. Now a flood of miracles began to be reported, and the cult of St Thomas began to take on a more directed character.

St Thomas of Canterbury

The most important single individual in the transformation of a
popular miracle-cult into the universally acknowledged cult of
St Thomas, martyr of Canterbury, was John of Salisbury. In the
spring of 1171 he wrote to his friend John, bishop of Poitiers, once
a clerk in Archbishop Theobald's household. This long letter,
called *Ex Insperato*, was meant to be circulated widely and its ulti-
mate target was the papal curia. It represents the earliest extended
case for why Thomas ought to be recognized as a saint. According
to the twelfth-century canonization procedure, there were three
criteria for martyrdom: the penalty (*poena*), the miracles (*signa*)
and the cause (*causa*). The first two had been demonstrated clearly
of Thomas, but the case had yet to be made fully for the third.
John made the point that papal recognition of Thomas's sanctity
should be forthcoming, and swiftly, as the power of such popular
acclaim as was being witnessed in Canterbury would wait for
the authority of no man. And John backed up his bid with a
statement of Thomas's qualities as precise and well structured
as a legal brief.

John's letter includes the earliest surviving account of
Thomas's murder. He describes Thomas's altercation with the
knights, his steadfast refusal to flee and his charge to spare his
followers, his last words in which he commended himself and his
cause to God and the saints, the brutal onslaught and the martyr's
courageous demeanour in his last moments. John also describes
how the knights plundered the archbishop's palace, and how the
monks discovered the hairshirt as they prepared Thomas's body
for burial. He imbues Thomas's every last step with meaning:

Take note too where his sacrifice was made. Yes, in the
church which is the kingdom's head, the mother in Christ
of all others in the kingdom, before the altar, among

his fellow priests, and in the ranks of the monks, whom
the shouts of the armed assassins had drawn together
to witness the pitiful and tremendous drama.

He had long shown himself as a living sacrifice, crucifying the
flesh in prayers, vigils and fasting, in wearing the hairshirt and
baring his back to the whip: 'He had been used to offer Christ's
body and blood upon the altar: and now, prostrate at the altar's
foot, he offered his own blood shed by the hands of evil men.'
Thomas was not in fact killed before the high altar, as implied
here, but this is the image that would be reiterated in literary
and visual representations of Thomas's murder: of the priest who
was accustomed to sacrifice on the altar presenting himself as a
sacrifice for the benefit of his church.

John's is also the earliest report we have of Thomas's veneration as a saint. He refers to 'the glorious martyr Thomas,
archbishop of Canterbury, who lights up not only his own church
but both the English provinces with many mighty wonders',
and he goes on to describe the situation currently in Canterbury.
Echoing the account of the aftermath of the crucifixion in
Matthew's gospel, John writes:

> In the place where Thomas suffered, and where he lay the
> night through, before the high altar, awaiting burial, and
> where he was buried at last, the palsied are cured, the
> blind see, the deaf hear, the dumb speak, the lame walk,
> folk suffering from fevers are cured, the lepers are cleansed,
> those possessed of a devil are freed, and the sick are made
> whole from all manner of disease, blasphemers taken over
> by the devil are put to confusion.[33]

But John's account of Thomas's death and posthumous miracles,
though significant, only occupies half of the letter. The first half

of the letter focuses not on the martyrdom and glorious aftermath but the life that went before. As John puts it, 'If the case
[*causa*] makes the martyr, as every wise man must think, what
could be juster and more holy than his?' Thomas, says John,
scorned riches and all the world's glory, put Christ's love before
friends and family, submitted to exile and laid himself open to
peril and poverty:

> He fought to the death to preserve his God's laws and to
> make nought abuses which came from ancient tyrants; nor
> – after a single fall when he was trapped by his enemies'
> guile – could he be induced by any compromise to pledge
> himself against any of the demands made to him without
> adding in every case 'saving God's honour and the Church's
> good name'. He extended his exile into a seventh year,
> following in the footsteps of Christ and the apostles, his
> spirit neither broken by fortune's onslaught nor weakened
> by charm or flattery.[34]

John concludes by asking 'whether it is safe, without papal
authority, to address him in celebration of Mass and other public
prayers among the catalogue of martyrs, as one with control over
salvation'. As he awaits such an answer, he suggests that it would
be wise to revere as a martyr one whom God deigns to honour as
a martyr. In other words, the evidence of Thomas's sanctity, as
displayed at Canterbury, should be all that is needed to confirm
his place among the martyrs of the Church.[35]

   Official recognition of Thomas's sanctity arrived very quickly.
Within a few months of the murder, once the ground had been
set by John of Salisbury, Herbert of Bosham and other influential friends, the monks of Canterbury sent a delegation to the
pope seeking Thomas's canonization. Around autumn 1171 legates came to Canterbury to investigate the miracles and they

seem to have returned a positive report to the curia. Finally on
21 February 1173 the pope officially declared Thomas a saint
and martyr and ordered the universal celebration of his feast.[36]

At the same time, the monks of Canterbury were beginning
to make the cult of St Thomas their own. Benedict of Peterborough was designated to record miracles at the shrine from
around Pentecost, May 1171, and about a year later he was joined
in the task by William of Canterbury. They wrote down accounts
that they had been told by pilgrims of how they or those close

Pilgrims on the road to Thomas Becket's tomb, 13th century, stained
glass, Canterbury Cathedral.

to them had experienced the martyr's miraculous power, whether at the tomb or elsewhere. They told of cures for all kinds of ailments – blindness, paralysis, leprosy, demonic possession – and how Thomas even brought the dead back to life. There are stories of sailors preserved from shipwreck, children saved from accidents, rich and poor rewarded by their prayers or by their contact with the martyr's relics, as well as miracles of vengeance against those who scoffed at the archbishop's sanctity. Thomas's adult life was lived in a male environment among the social elite, but in these miracle accounts it is those who seldom find a place in his life story who are prominent: women, children, the poor and sick of Canterbury and beyond. These miracle accounts are valuable testimony to beliefs, to medical practice and to the ordinary lives of people in twelfth-century England. In 1173 Benedict collected his recorded miracles into a huge volume, and over the following years William produced an even larger collection, comprising reports of miracles from far and wide.

In the early 1170s, too, John of Salisbury began the work of collecting and sorting the archbishop's correspondence, a task that was brought to fruition by Alan of Tewkesbury. Within a few years of Thomas's death, numerous Lives of St Thomas had appeared, including those by John of Salisbury, Edward Grim, the monks Benedict and William, William fitz Stephen, Guernes of Pont-Sainte-Maxence and various anonymous writers. The longest and most ambitious, by Herbert of Bosham, would be produced in the 1180s. The memorialization of the martyr was also enhanced by an act of God. In 1174 a fire in the eastern end of Canterbury Cathedral destroyed part of the choir and allowed the monks to embark on an ambitious rebuilding programme, supported by the generous and ongoing donations of pilgrims to the shrine. Under the guidance of a French architect, this part of the cathedral was reconstructed in the new Gothic style, and in the 1180s the Trinity Chapel was rebuilt and decorated with stained-glass windows in honour of St Thomas. On 7 July 1220 the relics of the martyr were translated from the crypt where they had lain for nearly fifty years to a new shrine in the apse of the cathedral.[37]

The King and the Saint

It took three days for the news of the murder to reach King Henry II at Argentan. A letter from a witness says that he shut himself away for three days, consumed nothing but almond milk and refused to show himself in public for fear that he would be blamed.[38] Yet despite this display of anguish, over the following weeks and months the king would show himself defiant. He sent an embassy to the papal court at Frascati, bearing a letter that blamed the archbishop for violating the peace and threatening the crown, only regretting that the knights 'fell upon him and – I say with grief – killed him'. Unfortunately for the king, two of Thomas's clerks, Alexander and Gunter, reached the curia before his embassy, and they carried with them letters from King Louis, Count Theobald of Blois and William, archbishop of Sens, demanding severe punishment of the offenders, including an interdict on Henry II's lands in France. The pope initially refused to see the royal envoys and they were only admitted when they swore on behalf of the king that he would abide by the pope's judgement. Now the pope issued a general excommunication of the murderers and those who abetted them, confirmed the interdict and Thomas's sentences on the ecclesiastics who had crowned the Young King, and forbade Henry II to enter a church until he had shown humility to the pope's legates.[39] Henry did not wait for the papal legates to arrive in Normandy. Some of his vassals had recently carved out territories for themselves in Ireland and Henry did not delay to cross over the Irish Sea to settle the volatile situation there in his favour. He spent the winter of 1171–2 in Ireland, where he laid the foundations for centuries of English rule.

It was around this time that the murderers began to make moves towards penance. Although in the days after the murder the knights flaunted their deed to the point of returning to Canterbury and threatening the monks, it would not take long for them to see the tide changing. They took refuge at the royal castle of Knaresborough in Yorkshire, which was in the custody of Hugh de Morville. They reportedly came to be shunned by neighbours, though they did not suffer any immediate reprisals from the king, who continued to allow them to hunt in his forests. The first signs of remorse, or fear, are evident in generous gifts recorded from the knights to various churches. William de Tracy seems to have been the first to accept penance, as he is found in Rome in the winter of 1171–2, and the others may have followed soon after. The pope sentenced the four to a public penance of fourteen years fighting in the Holy Land, in addition to the private penace they should do every day in fasting, prayer and almsgiving. Herbert claimed that none of them ever returned to England, and recent research suggests that they did indeed all die abroad.[40]

Finally the king returned to Normandy where he met the papal legates, Cardinals Albert and Theodwin. On 21 May 1172 at Avranches, after some negotiations, he swore on the gospels that he had neither ordered nor willed the death of the archbishop, a tragedy that he grieved more than the death of his parents, but accepted that his rash words had led to it, and he committed himself to carry out whatever satisfaction the cardinals would demand of him. The penance imposed obliged the king to support two hundred knights for the defence of Jerusalem for a year, to go on crusade himself by summer 1173 and to remove any evil customs. Finally, he was led to the door of the cathedral where he knelt before the cardinals, who absolved him and received him into the Church.[41] Henry would never in fact go on crusade, and he had this sentence commuted to the foundation of certain churches in honour of the martyr.

For Henry II, it might have seemed that the storm had passed. But in fact, the taint left by the murder of Thomas Becket would never be removed, and although the remaining eighteen years of his reign would include many successes, he would never again be the indomitable figure that he was before. In 1173 Henry II faced the greatest challenge to his position to date, when his wife Eleanor, his sons Henry, Richard and Geoffrey, the kings of France and Scotland, the count of Flanders, and many of his leading barons on both sides of the sea united in rebellion against him. Each had their own motives for rebelling, but their reason for choosing this moment is clear – the new vulnerability that attached itself to the king on account of his association with Thomas's murder. And it was to the cause of St Thomas that Henry the Young King appealed when he wrote to Pope Alexander justifying taking up arms against his father. In this letter he claims to be moved above all by the posthumous fate of his father and teacher, Thomas. Those who killed him have not faced royal justice, new prelates have been appointed from among those who persecuted Thomas during his life and the royal customs on account of which he died have not been abolished properly.[42] This was blatant propaganda: the Young King had been complicit in many of the outrages of which the archbishop had complained, and he was driven to rebellion more by his father's refusal to assign him a clear role than by any concern for ecclesiastical liberties. Rallying around the memory of St Thomas, the rebels conducted a multi-pronged campaign against Henry II that lasted over a year. But in the end it was Henry II who triumphed, and he did so with the aid of the martyr of Canterbury.

Already by the summer of 1174 Henry's strategic choices, his command of financial resources and his well-trained forces had helped to shift the advantage in his favour. But from the point of view of contemporary commentators, the reason for his eventual victory lay elsewhere: in his reconciliation with St Thomas. The king, who had been campaigning in Normandy, crossed the Channel and made for Canterbury on 12 July. He dismounted and travelled the last couple of miles on foot, and when he reached the city he took off his shoes and travelled barefoot and in ordinary clothes to the cathedral. There he fell on his knees and prayed, and when he reached the place where Thomas had been killed he covered the spot with tears and kisses. Reaching the tomb he prostrated his entire body before it, flooding the marble with tears. There he made a public confession before the monks, that if he had not ordered nor willed the murder, he was guilty on account of the words that had provoked it. He made offerings of gold and silk and promised an endowment to the monks. And then, with his outer clothes removed, he leaned his head and shoulders into one of the openings of the tomb, and was whipped five times by each of the bishops present, and three times by each of the eighty monks present. The whole night he spent in prayer and fasting at the tomb.[43]

On the morning of 13 July, just as the king was completing his pilgrimage to the martyr at Canterbury, at Alnwick near the Scottish border, King William of Scotland wandered into an ambush and was captured by Henry II's men. William's capture precipitated the end of the revolt, and peace was agreed on 30 September. To contemporaries, this was no coincidence. Edward Grim saw the rebellion as divine scourging of the king for his sins against Thomas, but claimed that the martyr, seeking not the death of the sinner but his conversion, brought the king to penance. Now that he had made satisfaction to the martyr, he was rewarded with victory. This narrative came to be widely disseminated and accepted in the following years. Just as the son rebelled against the father but was restored to his favour once peace was

Henry II's penance at Thomas Becket's tomb, 13th century, stained glass, Canterbury Cathedral.

restored, so Henry II was forgiven and reconciled to his spiritual father, Thomas. In effect, the cult of St Thomas was appropriated by Henry II. The penance at Canterbury helped to draw the line under the Becket dispute, and lay the foundations for Thomas's establishment as a national saint. The king's daughters took this further. His daughter Matilda and her husband Henry the Lion, duke of Saxony, made generous donations to churches dedicated to St Thomas, and had themselves depicted in portraiture under the approving gaze of both Henry II and the martyr. Eleanor, married to King Alfonso VIII of Castile, brought the cult of St Thomas to Spain, founding several churches dedicated to the martyr. And Joanna, married to King William II of Sicily, made various dedications to St Thomas, including the prominent placement of the martyr in a mosaic programme at Monreale Cathedral.[44]

Afterlife

'The world could not be silent about the passion of the most blessed Thomas,' wrote one anonymous writer in the aftermath of the murder, 'because even had men been silent, rocks and stones would have cried out.'[45] While it is true that most cried out in acclamation of the new martyr, there remained some dissenting voices. This is evident in the many stories of miraculous vengeance against scoffers, and of those who converted to faith in the martyr when they had been shown a sign. There also survives a report of a debate at Paris between certain theologians soon after Thomas's death. One made the case that Thomas was a true martyr by virtue of dying for the liberty of the Church, but another argued that he was a traitor worthy of death, 'if not such a death'.[46] A more nuanced position was taken by the Augustinian canon William of Newburgh, who wrote a history of England in the 1190s. William accepted Thomas's sanctity and criticized King Henry, but he said that he could not approve of his actions, even if they proceeded from praiseworthy zeal, because they brought no profit and only trouble.[47]

On the other hand, there were some veterans of the struggle who complained that the victory was not all that it had seemed, and that Thomas's real principles had been forgotten – that Thomas had become a miracle-worker appealing to all, rather than a righteous fighter for the truth. Gilbert of London, Roger of York and the others who had stood against Thomas had done their penance and continued in office. Thomas's successors as archbishops of Canterbury, and other ecclesiastics too, would be quick to invoke him as a symbol of triumphant struggle against royal overreach. Yet few showed much willingness to follow Thomas's political approach. Herbert of Bosham complained that the prelates of England every day adored the relics of Thomas's dead body but spurned his 'living relics' – including his former clerk – and ignored the cause for which he had died. He wrote his biography of St Thomas as a model to the archbishop's successors, 'so that as he did, you ought to do the same'.[48]

A saint, a traitor, a symbol, a model: these are some of the ways that Thomas has been seen. Others have contended that Thomas defies definition, and his true character will always elude us.[49] If so, this may be simply because we know too much about him. Other famous individuals from the Middle Ages often appear to us in one dimension on account of a dearth of contemporary witness or the layers of accumulated legend. Thomas on the other hand speaks to us in his own voice, and many of those who knew him chose to write about what he did, how he lived and what kind of a person he was. There is so much information that inconsistency, contradictions and complexities inevitably reveal themselves, and no amount of mythmaking can cover them over. But even if other aspects of his character are hard to pin down, one is clear: Thomas provoked strong reactions. From the scorn and jealousy of the other young men at court to the admiration and praise of the king, and from the exasperation and anger of his political enemies to the acclaim of the pilgrims to Canterbury, Thomas could not be ignored. In death and life he would divide people, but he would always capture their attention.

CHRONOLOGY

	October: At the royal council of Westminster Thomas and Henry clash over the issue of 'criminous clerks'
1164	January: At the royal council of Clarendon, Thomas is pressed to accept the 'ancestral customs of the realm', but rejects them when written down as the Constitutions of Clarendon
	October: Thomas is brought to trial at Northampton, and subsequently flees into exile in France
	November: Thomas has an audience with Pope Alexander III at Sens, and settles at the monastery of Pontigny
1165	Pope Alexander III returns to Rome
1166	12 June: Thomas issues excommunications and anathemas against his enemies at Vézelay
	July: Gilbert Foliot, bishop of London, writes his letter *Multiplicem nobis* denouncing Thomas's actions
	November: Thomas moves from Pontigny to Sens
1167	November: Peace conference at Planches
1169	January: The peace conference at Montmirail fails when Thomas refuses to submit his case to the king's mercy except 'saving God's honour'
	13 April: At Clairvaux Thomas excommunicates the bishops of London and Salisbury, and others who have violated the rights of Canterbury
	November: The peace conference at Montmartre fails when Henry refuses to grant Thomas the kiss of peace
1170	June: Henry II's son, Henry 'the Young King', is crowned at Westminster in Thomas's absence
	July: Peace is made at Fréteval and Thomas is allowed to return to Canterbury
	November: Thomas suspends from office the bishops involved in the coronation of the Young King and renews the excommunication of the bishops of London and Salisbury
	1 December: Thomas returns to England
	Mid-December: The censured bishops present their complaints about Thomas to the king at Bur-le-Roi in Normandy. The king's angry words prompt four knights to set out for Canterbury
	25 December: Thomas preaches in Canterbury Cathedral and issues further sentences against his enemies

	29 December: Thomas is murdered in Canterbury Cathedral
1171	April: Thomas's tomb is opened to the public, leading to growing numbers of pilgrims and reports of miracles
1172	21 May: Henry II submits to the cardinals at Avranches and promises satisfaction for his role in Thomas's murder
1173	21 February: Thomas is canonized as a saint by Pope Alexander III
	King Henry II faces a large-scale rebellion involving his sons Henry, Richard and Geoffrey, his wife Queen Eleanor, and the kings of France and Scotland
1174	12 July: King Henry II does penance at St Thomas's shrine in Canterbury
	September: fire seriously damages Canterbury Cathedral
1180–84	Canterbury Cathedral is rebuilt with chapels dedicated to housing the shrine and relics of St Thomas
1220	7 July: Thomas's body is translated to a new shrine
1538	King Henry VIII has Thomas's cult suppressed and his shrine destroyed

REFERENCES

Introduction

1 The Lives, miracles and letters are printed in their original Latin in James C. Robertson, ed., *Materials for the History of Thomas Becket*, 7 vols, Rolls Series (London, 1875–9) [hereafter MTB]. Thomas's correspondence is in Anne Duggan, ed. and trans., *The Correspondence of Thomas Becket, Archbishop of Canterbury, 1162–1170*, 2 vols (Oxford, 2000) [hereafter CTB]. For the French verse Life, see Guernes de Pont-Sainte-Maxence, *La Vie de S. Thomas le Martyr*, ed. Emanuel Walberg (Paris, 1922); and *Garnier's Becket*, trans. Janet Shirley (Chichester, 1975; repr. Felinfach, 1996). The Icelandic Saga, with English translation, is published in *Thómas Saga Erkibyskups*, ed. Eríkur Magnússon, 2 vols, Rolls Series (London, 1875–83). Extracts from the Lives are translated in Michael Staunton, ed. and trans., *The Lives of Thomas Becket* (Manchester, 2001) and George W. Greenaway, ed. and trans., *The Life and Death of Thomas Becket* (London, 1961).
2 The most authoritative modern scholarly biographies of Thomas Becket are Frank Barlow, *Thomas Becket*, 2nd edn (London, 1997), and Anne Duggan, *Thomas Becket* (London, 2004). Also recommended are David Knowles, *Thomas Becket* (London, 1970) and John Guy, *Thomas Becket: Warrior, Priest, Rebel* (New York, 2012).

1 Thomas of London

1 Robertson, ed., MTB, II, pp. 356–8; III, pp. 13–14; IV, pp. 3–5, 81–2; Guernes de Pont-Sainte-Maxence, *La Vie de S. Thomas le Martyr*, ed. Emanuel Walberg (Paris, 1922), vv. 171–200.
2 CTB, I, no. 95, pp. 402–5; no. 96, pp. 430–33; MTB, IV, pp. 27–8.
3 On Thomas's early life see especially Lewis B. Radford, *Thomas of London before His Consecration* (Cambridge, 1894).
4 MTB, I, p. 408; II, p. 356; III, pp. 14–15; IV, pp. 3, 81.
5 On the difficulty of dating the year of Thomas's birth see Frank Barlow, *Thomas Becket*, 2nd edn (London, 1997), p. 281.

6 *MTB*, II, pp. 453–8.

7 See Barlow, *Thomas Becket*, p. 12.

8 *MTB*, IV, p. 7; see II, pp. 302–3.

9 See Barlow, *Becket*, pp. 13–14.

10 *MTB*, III, p. 8.

11 Richard of Devizes, *The Chronicle of Richard of Devizes of the Time of King Richard the First*, ed. John T. Appleby (London, 1963), pp. 64–5.

12 *MTB*, III, pp. 14–15; *Thómas Saga Erkibyskups*, ed. Eríkur Magnússon, 2 vols, Rolls Series (London, 1875–83), I, pp. 18–21.

13 *MTB*, III, pp. 2–13.

14 *MTB*, III, pp. 4–5.

15 *MTB*, III, p. 8.

16 *MTB*, III, p. 9.

17 *MTB*, III, pp. 11–12.

18 *MTB* II, pp. 360–61; IV, p. 6; Guernes, *Vie de S. Thomas le Martyr*, vv. 206–29; *Saga*, I, pp. 30–35.

19 Orderic Vitalis, *Historia ecclesiastica*, ed. and trans. Marjorie Chibnall, 6 vols (Oxford, 1968–80), VI, p. 16.

20 *MTB*, III, p. 14; *Saga*, I, pp. 20–23.

21 See Charles H. Haskins, *The Renaissance of the Twelfth Century* (Cambridge, MA, 1927); Beryl Smalley, *The Becket Conflict and the Schools* (Oxford, 1973).

22 *MTB*, I, p. 3; II, p. 359; IV, p. 8.

23 *Saga*, I, pp. 28–9.

24 *MTB*, III, p. 17.

25 *MTB*, III, p. 165.

26 *MTB*, III, pp. 163–5; see Luke 2:52.

27 *MTB*, III, p. 165.

28 *MTB*, I, p. 3; II, p. 361; Guernes, *Vie de S. Thomas le Martyr*, vv. 241–5.

29 *MTB*, III, p. 14.

30 *MTB*, IV, p. 8.

31 Robert Bartlett, *England under the Norman and Angevin Kings, 1075–1225* (Oxford, 2000), pp. 377–8.

32 *MTB*, II, p. 303; III, p. 167.

33 *MTB*, II, p. 361; III, p. 15; IV, pp. 9–10; Guernes, *Vie de S. Thomas le Martyr*, vv. 246–59; *Saga*, I, pp. 32–5.

34 On Theobald, see Avrom Saltman, *Theobald, Archbishop of Canterbury* (New York, 1969).

35 On the history of Canterbury, see William Urry, *Canterbury under the Angevin Kings* (London, 1967) and Patrick Collinson, Nigel

Ramsey and Margaret Sparks, eds, *A History of Canterbury Cathedral*, revd edn (Oxford, 2002).

36 See Saltman, *Theobald*, pp. 165–77.

37 *MTB*, II, p. 362; IV, p. 10; Guernes, *Vie de S. Thomas le Martyr*, vv. 256–60.

38 See Barlow, *Becket*, p. 29.

39 *MTB*, III, p. 17.

40 Ibid.

41 See James A. Brundage, *Medieval Canon Law* (London, 1995).

42 *MTB*, III, p. 16; see II, p. 308.

43 See Judith Green, *Henry I, King of England and Duke of Normandy* (Cambridge, 2009) and Marjorie Chibnall, *The Empress Matilda* (Oxford, 1993).

44 *Peterborough Chronicle* a. 1137.

45 See Edmund King, *King Stephen* (New Haven, CT, 2010) and Edmund King, ed., *The Anarchy of King Stephen's Reign* (Oxford, 1994).

46 On Henry II's life and rule, see in particular Wilfred L. Warren, *Henry II* (London, 1973) and Christopher Harper-Bill and Nicholas Vincent, eds, *Henry II: New Interpretations* (Woodbridge, 2007).

47 On Eleanor see Bonnie Wheeler and John C. Parsons, eds, *Eleanor of Aquitaine: Lord and Lady* (New York, 2003); and Ralph V. Turner, *Eleanor of Aquitaine: Queen of France, Queen of England* (New Haven, CT, 2009).

48 John of Salisbury, *Historia pontificalis*; *CTB*, I, no. 153, pp. 718–21; *MTB*, II, p. 303; III, p. 16; IV, p. 10; Guernes, *Vie de S. Thomas le Martyr*, vv. 261–5; *Saga*, I, pp. 38–9.

49 See Saltman, *Theobald*, pp. 37–41.

2 Royal Chancellor

1 Robertson, ed., *MTB*, III, p. 25.

2 *MTB*, III, pp. 18–19.

3 William Stubbs, ed., *Select Charters and Other Illustrations of English Constitutional History* (Oxford, 1870), p. 158.

4 See Emilie Amt, *The Accession of Henry II in England: Royal Government Restored, 1149–1159* (Woodbridge, 1993).

5 See the descriptions by Peter of Blois in *MTB*, VII, no. 800, pp. 571–6, by Gerald of Wales in *Expugnatio Hibernica: The Conquest of Ireland*, ed. A. B. Scott and F. X. Martin (Dublin, 1978), pp. 124–33, and Walter Map, *De Nugis Curialium: Courtiers' Trifles*, ed. M. R. James, rev. C.N.L. Brooke and R.A.B. Mynors (Oxford, 1983), pp. 237–42.

6 *MTB*, III, pp. 17–18; see also IV, p. 12.

7 On these developments, see Wilfred L. Warren, *The Governance of Norman and Angevin England, 1086–1272* (London, 1987) and Michael Clanchy, *From Memory to Written Record: England, 1066–1307*, 3rd edn (Oxford, 2012).

8 'The Dialogue Concerning the Exchequer', preface, in *Select Charters*, ed. Stubbs, p. 168.

9 Walter Map, *De Nugis Curialium*, pp. 2–3.

10 *MTB*, III, pp. 20–23.

11 *MTB*, III, pp. 29–31.

12 *MTB*, III, pp. 24–5.

13 *MTB*, II, p. 304; IV, p. 11.

14 *MTB*, III, pp. 23–4.

15 *MTB*, II, pp. 304–5.

16 *MTB*, IV, p. 12.

17 *MTB*, I, p. 6; Guernes de Pont-Sainte-Maxence, *La Vie de S. Thomas le Martyr*, ed. Emanuel Walberg (Paris, 1922), vv. 301–4.

18 *MTB*, I, p. 5.

19 *MTB*, II, p. 364; see Isaiah 1:4.

20 See John Gillingham, *The Angevin Empire* (London, 1984).

21 *MTB*, III, pp. 33–4, 175–6; Guernes, *Vie de S. Thomas le Martyr*, vv. 346–60; John of Salisbury, *Policraticus*, viii, 25, in Clement Webb, ed., *Policratici, sive, De nugis curialium et vestigiis philosophorum* (Oxford, 1909), p. 424; *CTB*, I, no. 109, pp. 504–5.

22 *MTB*, III, p. 34.

23 *MTB*, III, p. 35.

24 *MTB*, II, p. 365.

25 *MTB*, V, no. 8, p. 11.

26 *MTB*, III, pp. 25–6.

27 *MTB*, III, p. 181.

28 Gratian 1.23.2 (col. 79), quoted by Robert Bartlett, *England under the Norman and Angevin Kings, 1075–1225* (Oxford, 2000), p. 395.

29 *MTB*, III, p. 182; see also IV, p. 85.

30 *MTB*, I, pp. 6–9; II, pp. 305–6, 365–7; III, pp. 35–6, 180–85; IV, pp. 14–19.

31 *MTB*, II, pp. 305–6.

32 *MTB*, IV, pp. 84–7. See Michael Staunton, 'Eadmer's *Vita Anselmi*: A Reinterpretation', *Journal of Medieval History*, XXIII (1997), pp. 1–14 (pp. 4–9).

33 *MTB*, III, pp. 185–6; see Matthew 25:14–30.

34 MTB, IV, p. 19.

35 Matthew 21:19; see CTB, I, no. 109, pp. 504–7.

36 MTB, III, p. 185.

37 MTB, III, pp. 37, 41.

3 Conversion and Conflict

1 See John W. Coakley, 'The Conversion of St Francis and the Writing of Christian Biography, 1228–1263', *Franciscan Studies*, LXXII (2014), pp. 27–71.

2 Robertson, ed., MTB, II, p. 368; see I, p. 11.

3 MTB, II, pp. 369–71.

4 MTB, I, p. 10.

5 Ibid.; III, p. 37; see Seneca, *Epistles*, no. 5, in Seneca, *Epistles*, vol. I: *Epistles 1–65*, trans. Richard M. Gummere. Loeb Classical Library 75 (Cambridge, MA, 1917), pp. 20–21. See also MTB, II, pp. 306, 368–9; III, pp. 193–7; IV, pp. 20–21, 89; Guernes de Pont-Sainte-Maxence, *La Vie de S. Thomas le Martyr*, ed. Emanuel Walberg (Paris, 1922), vv. 561–95.

6 See Frank Barlow, *Thomas Becket*, 2nd edn (London, 1997), p. 75.

7 MTB, II, pp. 345–6.

8 MTB, III, p. 21.

9 David Knowles, 'Thomas Becket: A Character Study', in Knowles, *The Historian and Character, and Other Essays* (Cambridge, 1963), pp. 98–128 (pp. 110, 100); David Knowles, *Thomas Becket* (London, 1970), p. 54.

10 See Michael Staunton, 'Thomas Becket's Conversion', *Anglo-Norman Studies*, XXI (1999), pp. 193–211.

11 MTB, I, pp. 10–11; III, p. 39.

12 MTB, II, p. 308.

13 MTB, III, pp. 198–238 (p. 198).

14 MTB, III, p. 204.

15 MTB, III, p. 225.

16 MTB, III, p. 226.

17 MTB, III, p. 227.

18 MTB, III, p. 230.

19 MTB, III, p. 231.

20 MTB, I, p. 12; Guernes, *Vie de S. Thomas le Martyr*, vv. 740–50.

21 MTB, III, pp. 42–3, 250–52.

22 MTB, III, pp. 252–3.

23 MTB, III, pp. 253–5, 261; see Luke 2:22–40; Ecclesiastes 3:1, 4:8.

24 *MTB*, I, p. 12; II, pp. 373–4; IV, pp. 23–4; Guernes, *Vie de S. Thomas le Martyr*, vv. 751–70.

25 *MTB*, III, p. 43.

26 See Peter D. Clarke, 'Excommunication and Interdict', in *The Cambridge History of Medieval Canon Law*, ed. Anders Winroth and John C. Wei (Cambridge, 2022), pp. 550–70.

27 *MTB*, I, pp. 12–13; II, pp. 374–6; III, pp. 45, 265–66; IV, pp. 24–5; Guernes, *La Vie de S. Thomas le Martyr*, vv. 771–825.

28 See Charles Duggan, 'The Becket Dispute and the Criminous Clerks', *Bulletin of the Institute of Historical Research*, xxxv/91 (1962), pp. 1–28, and Beryl Smalley, *The Becket Conflict and the Schools* (Oxford, 1973), pp. 122–33.

29 On the Council of Westminster see *MTB*, I, p. 13; II, pp. 310, 375–7; III, pp. 261–75; IV, pp. 25–7, 95–7, 201–5; Guernes, *Vie de S. Thomas le Martyr*, vv. 826–50; *Thómas Saga Erkibyskups*, ed. Eríkur Magnússon, 2 vols, Rolls Series (London, 1875–83), I, pp. 146–57.

30 Jerome's commentary on Nahum 1:9.

31 *MTB*, III, p. 261.

32 *Eadmeri Historia Novorum in Anglia*, ed. Martin Rule, Rolls Series (London, 1884), p. 35.

33 See Ian S. Robinson, *Authority and Resistance in the Investiture Contest* (Manchester, 1978) and Uta-Renate Blumenthal, *The Investiture Controversy: Church and Monarchy from the Ninth to the Twelfth Century* (Philadelphia, PA, 1988).

34 *MTB*, III, p. 268; see Psalms 148:8. See also *MTB*, II, pp. 387–8; IV, p. 26.

35 See David Knowles, *The Episcopal Colleagues of Thomas Becket* (Cambridge, 1951).

36 *MTB*, I, pp. 13–15; II, pp. 377–9; IV, pp. 30–32; Guernes, *Vie de S. Thomas le Martyr*, vv. 851–910.

37 *MTB*, III, p. 277; IV, pp. 32–3.

38 For the Council, see *MTB*, I, pp. 15–23; II, pp. 311–12, 379–83; III, pp. 46–8, 278–92; IV, pp. 33–7, 99–103; Guernes, *Vie de S. Thomas le Martyr*, vv. 920–1035; *Saga*, I, pp. 160–77; Duggan, ed. and trans., *CTB*, I, no. 109, pp. 508–13.

39 *MTB*, IV, p. 36.

40 *MTB*, IV, p. 37.

41 The Constitutions are printed in Dorothy Whitelock, Martin Brett and C.N.L. Brooke, eds, *Councils and Synods with Other Documents Relating to the English Church*, I: *AD 871–1204*, Part 2, 1066–1204 (Oxford, 1981), no. 159, pp. 877–83.

42 *MTB*, III, p. 287.

43 Clause 5, *Councils and Synods*, p. 878.

44 Clause 7, *Councils and Synods*, p. 880.

45 Clause 4, *Councils and Synods*, p. 879.

46 Clause 8, *Councils and Synods*, p. 880.

47 *MTB*, III, pp. 47–8.

48 *MTB*, III, p. 100.

49 See Michael T. Clanchy, *From Memory to Written Record: England, 1066–1307* (Oxford, 1979).

50 *CTB*, no. 109, pp. 510–11.

51 *MTB*, II, p. 324.

52 *MTB*, III, p. 292.

4 Trial and Exile

1 See Frank Barlow, *Thomas Becket*, 2nd edn (London, 1997), p. 106.

2 Robertson, ed., *MTB*, I, pp. 30–31; II, pp. 390–91; III, pp. 50–51, 296–8; IV, pp. 40–41; Guernes de Pont-Sainte-Maxence, *La Vie de S. Thomas le Martyr*, ed. Emanuel Walberg (Paris, 1922), vv. 1400–1460.

3 *MTB*, III, p. 68.

4 I mainly follow William fitz Stephen's account: *MTB*, III, pp. 49–68. See also *MTB*, I, pp. 30–40; II, pp. 326–33, 391–8; III, pp. 296–312; IV, pp. 41–52; Guernes, *Vie de S. Thomas le Martyr*, vv. 1383–1970.

5 *MTB*, II, p. 392.

6 See Anne Duggan, *Thomas Becket* (London, 2004), p. 66.

7 *MTB*, III, p. 55.

8 *MTB*, III, pp. 55–6.

9 Psalms 119:23 and 86.

10 *MTB*, III, p. 56.

11 *MTB*, III, pp. 56–7.

12 *MTB*, II, p. 394.

13 Luke 22:38.

14 *MTB*, III, p. 268; see also IV, p. 22.

15 *MTB*, III, p. 65.

16 Matthew 16:24.

17 See Martin Aurell, *The Plantagenet Empire, 1154–1224*, trans. D. Crouch (Harlow, 2007), pp. 244–8.

18 *MTB*, III, p. 63.

19 *MTB*, III, p. 64.

20 Ibid.; see Matthew 9:3.

21 *MTB*, III, p. 65.

22 *MTB*, III, p. 67.

23 See Duggan, *Thomas Becket*, p. 80.

24 *MTB*, III, p. 68.

25 *MTB*, III, p. 312.

26 Clause 4, in *Councils and Synods with Other Documents Relating to the English Church*, vol. I: AD 871–1204, Part 2, 1066–1204, ed. Dorothy Whitelock, Martin Brett and C.N.L. Brooke (Oxford, 1981), no. 159, p. 879.

27 John 10:10–11.

28 On Thomas's progress from Northampton to Sens, see *MTB*, I, pp. 40–43, 46; II, pp. 335–7, 399–403; III, pp. 70–74, 310–15, 318–35, 338–40; IV, pp. 52–61, 105–7; Guernes, *Vie de S. Thomas le Martyr*, vv. 1971–2150.

29 *MTB*, III, p. 325; see 2 Corinthians 5:17.

30 *MTB*, II, p. 335; IV, pp. 56–7.

31 Duggan, ed. and trans., *CTB*, I, no. 24, pp. 64–5.

32 *MTB*, III, pp. 407–8.

33 *MTB*, III, p. 332; Guernes, *Vie de S. Thomas le Martyr*, vv. 2161–330.

34 This account follows Alan of Tewkesbury: *MTB*, II, pp. 337–45. See also *MTB*, I, p. 46; II, pp. 402–4; III, pp. 72–6, 334–57; IV, pp. 60–65; *Thómas Saga Erkibyskups*, ed. Eríkur Magnússon, 2 vols, Rolls Series (London, 1875–83), I, pp. 270–313; Guernes, *Vie de S. Thomas le Martyr*, vv. 2331–90, 2546–60.

35 *MTB*, II, pp. 337–40.

36 *MTB*, II, pp. 340–42.

37 *MTB*, II, p. 342–3.

38 *MTB*, II, pp. 344–5.

39 See Mette B. Bruun, ed., *The Cambridge Companion to the Cistercian Order* (Cambridge, 2013).

40 On Thomas's asceticism in exile see *MTB*, I, p. 49; II, pp. 345–6, 412–13; III, pp. 76–7, 357–8, 376–9; IV, p. 64; Guernes, *Vie de S. Thomas le Martyr*, vv. 3891–80; *Saga*, I, pp. 312–19.

41 *MTB*, III, p. 358; see IV, p. 118; *CTB*, I, no. 42, pp. 172–3.

42 *MTB*, I, pp. 46–7; II, pp. 313–14, 404–5; III, pp. 75–6, 358–75; IV, pp. 64–5, 108; Guernes, *Vie de S. Thomas le Martyr*, vv. 2566–640.

43 *CTB*, I, no. 54, pp. 224–5.

44 *MTB*, III, p. 381.

45 *CTB*, I, no. 68, pp. 266–71; no. 74, pp. 292–9; no. 82, pp. 328–43.

46 *CTB*, I, no. 74, pp. 296–7; see Isaiah 10:1–12.

47 *CTB*, I, no. 82, pp. 340–41; see Psalms 73–4:22; Revelation 19:2.

48 *CTB*, I, no. 70, pp. 272–9; *MTB*, V, no. 173, pp. 329–31.

5 Thomas Alone

1 W. J. Millor and C.N.L. Brooke, eds, *The Letters of John of Salisbury*, vol. II: *The Later Letters* (Oxford, 1979) [hereafter *LJS*], no. 168, pp. 110–11; Robertson, ed., *MTB*, III, p. 392.

2 *MTB*, III, pp. 391–3; *CTB*, I, nos 76–81, pp. 302–29.

3 *MTB*, III, p. 392.

4 *LJS*, II, no. 168, pp. 112–15.

5 *MTB*, V, no. 204, pp. 403–8.

6 See Giles Constable, *Letters and Letter Collections*, Typologie des sources du Moyen Age occidental 17 (Turnhout, 1976).

7 *CTB*, I, no. 93, pp. 372–83.

8 See Psalms 74:22.

9 *CTB*, I, no. 95, pp. 388–425.

10 See Adrian Morey and C.N.L. Brooke, *Gilbert Foliot and His Letters* (Cambridge, 1965).

11 *CTB*, I, no. 96, pp. 426–41.

12 *CTB*, I, no. 109, pp. 498–537.

13 *MTB*, II, pp. 314–15, 413–15; III, pp. 83–4, 397–404; Guernes de Pont-Sainte-Maxence, *La Vie de S. Thomas le Martyr*, ed. Emanuel Walberg (Paris, 1922), vv. 3601–720; *Thómas Saga Erkibyskups*, ed. Eríkur Magnússon, 2 vols, Rolls Series (London, 1875–83), I, pp. 368–75.

14 *MTB*, III, p. 415.

15 *CTB*, I, no. 119, pp. 572–3.

16 *CTB*, I, no. 123, pp. 588–9.

17 *MTB*, III, pp. 408–12.

18 *MTB*, I, pp. 73–5; II, pp. 347–51, 416–17; III, pp. 96–7, 418–40; IV, pp. 113–14; VI, no. 451, pp. 488–90; Guernes, *Vie de S. Thomas le Martyr*, vv. 4071–190; *LJS*, no. 288, pp. 638–47.

19 *MTB*, III, pp. 438–40.

20 *MTB*, II, pp. 350–51.

21 *MTB*, VI, p. 122.

22 2 Samuel 23:8–38.

23 *MTB*, III, pp. 213–15.

24 See Michael Staunton, ed., *Herbert of Bosham: A Medieval Polymath* (Woodbridge, 2019).

25 *LJS*, no. 228, pp. 400–401.

26 See Michael Wilks, ed., *The World of John of Salisbury*, Studies in Church History 3 (Oxford, 1984).

27 *CTB*, II, nos 194–6, pp. 848–57.

28 *CTB*, II, no. 207, pp. 900–909; *MTB*, III, pp. 88–90.

29 *MTB*, I, pp. 53–5; VII, nos. 599–600, pp. 147–51.

30 *MTB*, III, pp. 97–8, 445–6.

31 See Martin Aurell, *The Plantagenet Empire, 1154–1224*, trans. D. Crouch (Harlow, 2007), pp. 248–51.

32 *CTB*, II, no. 266, pp. 1142–3; no. 285, pp. 1216–19.

33 *MTB*, III, pp. 103, 458; IV, p. 66. See Anne Duggan, 'The Coronation of the Young King in 1170', in Duggan, *Thomas Becket: Friends, Networks, Text and Cult* (Aldershot, 2007), pp. 165–78.

34 *MTB*, III, pp. 459–61.

35 *MTB*, VII, no. 628, pp. 210–12.

36 *MTB*, III, pp. 106–7.

37 *CTB*, II, no. 300, pp. 1260–79; *MTB*, III, pp. 107–12, 465–7.

38 *MTB*, III, pp. 111–16, 467–71.

39 *MTB*, III, p. 112.

40 *CTB*, II, no. 311, pp. 1302–9; see *LJS*, no. 304, pp. 714–19.

41 *MTB*, I, pp. 86–7; III, pp. 116–18, 471–6.

42 *MTB*, III, p. 117.

6 Murder

1 Robertson, ed., *MTB*, III, pp. 116, 113.

2 *MTB*, III, p. 117; see I, pp. 85–6; Guernes de Pont-Sainte-Maxence, *La Vie de S. Thomas le Martyr*, ed. Emanuel Walberg (Paris, 1922), vv. 4656–80.

3 *LJS*, no. 304, pp. 714–19.

4 *CTB*, II, no. 320, pp. 1334–5.

5 *MTB*, III, p. 148.

6 On Thomas's return and murder see William Urry, *Thomas Becket: His Last Days* (Stroud, 1999).

7 *MTB*, I, pp. 99–104; III, pp. 118–21, 476–80; IV, pp. 68–9, 124–5; Guernes, *Vie de S. Thomas le Martyr*, vv. 4716–55; *Thómas Saga Erkibyskups*, ed. Eríkur Magnússon, 2 vols, Rolls Series (London, 1875–83), I, pp. 488–501; *CTB*, II, no. 326, pp. 1344–55; *LJS*, II, no. 304, pp. 718–23.

8 *MTB*, I, pp. 105–19; III, pp. 121–7, 481–4; IV, p. 126; Guernes, *Vie de S. Thomas le Martyr*, vv. 4756–950; *Saga*, I, pp. 501–12; *LJS*, no. 304, pp. 722–3.

9 *MTB*, III, p. 484.

10 T. S. Eliot, *Murder in the Cathedral* (London, 1935), part 1, section 5, p. 44.

11 MTB, III, p. 486.

12 CTB, I, no. 112, pp. 542–3.

12 It derives from George, Lord Lyttelton, The History of the Life of King Henry the Second, 5 vols, new edn (London, 1777), vol. IV, p. 353.

13 MTB, I, pp. 105, 121–3; II, pp. 428–9; III, pp. 127–9, 481, 487; Guernes, Vie de S. Thomas le Martyr, vv. 5011–45.

14 See Nicholas Vincent, 'The Murderers of Thomas Becket', in Bischofsmord im Mittelalter: Murder of Bishops, ed. Natalie Fryde and Dirk Reitz (Göttingen, 2003), pp. 211–72.

15 The accounts of the murder are in MTB, I, pp. 127–36; II, pp. 1–16, 316–21, 430–39; III, pp. 132–47, 488–9, 491–514; IV, pp. 69–78, 128–32; Guernes, Vie de S. Thomas le Martyr, vv. 5161–691; Saga, I, p. 521–49; LJS, no. 305, pp. 724–33. They are compared and analysed by Edwin Abbott, St Thomas of Canterbury, His Death and Miracles, 2 vols (London, 1898), I, pp. 11–219. See also Jennifer O'Reilly, 'The Double Martyrdom of Thomas Becket: Hagiography or History?', Studies in Medieval and Renaissance History, 7 (1985), pp. 185–247.

16 MTB, II, pp. 430–39.

17 MTB, II, pp. 430–31.

18 MTB, II, pp. 431–3.

19 MTB, II, p. 9.

20 See Acts of the Christian Martyrs, ed. and trans. Henry Musurillo (Oxford, 1972).

21 MTB, II, pp. 433–5.

22 MTB, II, p. 435.

23 MTB, III, p. 139; see I, pp. 133–4.

24 MTB, II, pp. 435–6.

25 MTB, III, p. 140.

26 MTB, II, pp. 436–7.

27 MTB, I, p. 133; II, p. 12; III, pp. 141, 492–3; IV, p. 76.

28 LJS, nos 244, 300, pp. 486–7, 700–707.

29 MTB, II, pp. 16–17.

30 MTB, III, p. 150.

31 See Benedicta Ward, Miracles and the Medieval Mind: Theory, Record and Event, 1000–1215, 2nd edn (Aldershot, 1987); Rachel Koopmans, Wonderful to Relate: Miracle Stories and Miracle Collecting in High Medieval England (Philadelphia, PA, 2011); Robert Bartlett, Why Can the Dead Do Such Great Things? Saints and Worshippers from the Martyrs to the Reformation (Princeton, NJ, 2013).

33 LJS, no. 305, pp. 736–7.

34 *LJS*, no. 305, pp. 726–9.

35 *LJS*, no. 305, pp. 736–9.

36 *MTB*, VII, nos 784–6, pp. 545–50.

37 See Marie-Pierre Gelin and Paul Webster, eds, *The Cult of St Thomas Becket in the Plantagenet World, c. 1170–c. 1220* (Woodbridge, 2016) and Kay B. Slocum, *The Cult of Thomas Becket: History and Historiography through Eight Centuries* (Oxford, 2019).

38 *MTB*, VII, no. 738, pp. 438–9; I, 124–6; III, p. 542.

39 *MTB*, VII, no. 751, pp. 475–8.

40 Herbert of Bosham, *Liber Melorum*, in *Patrologia Latina*, ed. J.-P. Migne (Paris, 1893), CXC, cols 1303–4; Vincent, 'Murderers of Thomas Becket'.

41 See Anne Duggan, 'Diplomacy, Status, and Conscience: Henry II's Penance for Becket's Murder', in Duggan, *Friends, Networks, Texts and Cult*, pp. 265–90.

42 *Epistolae Henrici II*, no. 66, in *Recueil des historiens des Gaules et de la France*, ed. M. Bouquet et al., 24 vols (Paris, 1869–1904), vol. XVI, pp. 643–8.

43 *MTB*, II, pp. 444–8; see I, pp. 485–95; Herbert of Bosham, *Liber Melorum*, cols 1316–21.

44 See Colette Bowie, *The Daughters of Henry II and Eleanor of Aquitaine* (Brussels, 2014).

45 *MTB*, IV, p. 159.

46 Caesarius of Heisterbach, *Dialogus Miraculorum*, ed. Joseph Strange, 2 vols (Cologne, 1851), vol. II, pp. 139–40.

47 William of Newburgh, *Historia Rerum Anglicarum*, in *Chronicles of the Reigns of Stephen, Henry II and Richard*, ed. Richard Howlett, 4 vols, Rolls Series (London, 1884), vol. I, pp. 160–65.

48 Herbert of Bosham, *Liber Melorum*, cols 1403–4; *MTB*, III, p. 156.

49 David Knowles, 'Archbishop Thomas Becket: A Character Study', in Knowles, *The Historian and Character and Other Essays* (Cambridge, 1963), pp. 98–128.

SELECT BIBLIOGRAPHY

Primary

Douglas, David C., and George W. Greenaway, eds, *English Historical Documents*, vol. II: *1042–1189* (London, 1981)

Duggan, Anne, ed. and trans., *The Correspondence of Thomas Becket, Archbishop of Canterbury, 1162–1170*, 2 vols (Oxford, 2000)

Foliot, Gilbert, *The Letters and Charters of Gilbert Foliot*, ed. Adrian Morey and C.N.L. Brooke (Cambridge, 1967)

Greenaway, George W., ed. and trans., *The Life and Death of Thomas Becket* (London, 1961)

Guernes of Pont-Sainte-Maxence, *Garnier's Becket*, trans. Janet Shirley (Chichester, 1975; repr. Felinfach, 1996)

John of Salisbury, *The Letters of John of Salisbury*, ed. W. J. Millor and C.N.L. Brooke, 2 vols (Oxford, 1979)

Magnússon, Eríkur, ed., *Thómas Saga Erkibyskups*, 2 vols, Rolls Series (London, 1875–83)

Robertson, James C., ed., *Materials for the History of Thomas Becket*, 7 vols, Rolls Series (London, 1875–9)

Staunton, Michael, ed. and trans., *The Lives of Thomas Becket* (Manchester, 2001)

Whitelock, Dorothy, Martin Brett and C.N.L. Brooke, eds, *Councils and Synods with Other Documents Relating to the English Church*, I: *AD 871–1204, Part 2, 1066–1204* (Oxford, 1981)

Secondary

Abbott, Edwin, *St Thomas of Canterbury, His Death and Miracles*, 2 vols (London, 1898)

Aurell, Martin, *The Plantagenet Empire, 1154–1224*, trans. D. Crouch (Harlow, 2007)

Barlow, Frank, *The English Church, 1066–1154* (London, 1979)

—, *Thomas Becket*, 2nd edn (London, 1997)

Borenius, Tancred, *Thomas Becket in Art* (London, 1932)

Butler, J., *The Quest for Becket's Bones* (London, 1995)

Cheney, C. R., *From Becket to Langton* (Manchester, 1956)

De Beer, Lloyd, and Naomi Speakman, *Thomas Becket: Murder and the Making of a Saint* (London, 2020)

Duggan, Anne, *Thomas Becket: A Textual History of His Letters* (Oxford, 1980)

—, *Thomas Becket* (London, 2004)

—, *Thomas Becket: Friends, Networks, Text and Cult* (Aldershot, 2007)

Duggan, Charles, *Canon Law in Medieval England: The Becket Dispute and Decretal Collections* (London, 1982)

Foreville, Raymonde, ed., *Thomas Becket: Actes du Colloque International de Sédières, 19–24 août 1973* (Paris, 1975)

Gelin, Marie-Pierre, and Paul Webster, eds, *The Cult of St Thomas Becket in the Plantagenet World, c. 1170–c. 1220* (Woodbridge, 2016)

Guy, John, *Thomas Becket: Warrior, Priest, Rebel* (New York, 2012)

Harper-Bill, Christopher, and Nicholas Vincent, eds, *Henry II: New Interpretations* (Woodbridge, 2007)

Knowles, David, *The Episcopal Colleagues of Thomas Becket* (Cambridge, 1951)

—, 'Archbishop Thomas Becket: A Character Study', in Knowles, *The Historian and Character and Other Essays* (Cambridge, 1963), pp. 98–128

—, *Thomas Becket* (London, 1970)

Morey, Adrian, and C.N.L. Brooke, *Gilbert Foliot and His Letters* (Cambridge, 1965)

O'Reilly, Jennifer, 'The Double Martyrdom of Thomas Becket: Hagiography or History?', *Studies in Medieval and Renaissance History*, 7 (1985), pp. 185–247

Radford, Lewis B., *Thomas of London before His Consecration* (Cambridge, 1894)

Robertson, James C., *Becket, Archbishop of Canterbury: A Biography* (London, 1859)

Slocum, Kay B., *The Cult of Thomas Becket: History and Historiography through Eight Centuries* (Oxford, 2019)

Smalley, Beryl, *The Becket Conflict and the Schools* (Oxford, 1973)

Staunton, Michael, *Thomas Becket and His Biographers* (Woodbridge, 2007)

—, ed., *Herbert of Bosham: A Medieval Polymath* (Woodbridge, 2019)

Urry, William, *Thomas Becket: His Last Days* (Stroud, 1999)

Warren, Wilfrid L., *Henry II* (London, 1973)

Wilks, Michael., ed., *The World of John of Salisbury*, Studies in Church History 3 (Oxford, 1984)

ACKNOWLEDGEMENTS

Although I have long had an interest in the subject of Thomas Becket, and in the subject of biography, I never thought I would write a biography of Thomas Becket, so my first thanks are to Michael Leaman at Reaktion for giving me the opportunity to do so, and to Alex Ciobanu and Amy Salter for all their help in making it a reality. I would also like to thank the many students, colleagues and friends whose conversations with me over many years have made a great difference to my understanding of Thomas Becket and the world he lived in, including Haki Antonsson, Martin Aurell, Colette Bowie, Des Brennan, Stephen Church, Laura Cleaver, Edward Coleman, Christopher de Hamel, Leah Duffin, Anne Duggan, Gillian Evans, Herb Folpe, Jane Folpe, Tom James, Jitske Jasperse, Julie Kerr, Marisa Libbon, Théo Molines-Smyth, Colmán O'Clabaigh, Jennifer O'Reilly, Nicholas Paul, Gesine Oppitz-Trotman, Matthew Strickland, Karen Sullivan, Nicholas Vincent, Yuanding Wang, Björn Weiler, Emily Winkler.

PHOTO ACKNOWLEDGEMENTS

The author and publishers wish to express their thanks to the sources listed below for illustrative material and/or permission to reproduce it. Some locations of artworks are also given below, in the interest of brevity:

AdobeStock: p. 113 (photo Jean-Jacques Cordier); Alamy Stock Photo/ Heritage Image Partnership Ltd: pp. 10 (Ashmolean Museum, University of Oxford), 64 (Museum of London); Biblioteca Apostolica Vaticana, Vatican City (Cod. Vat. Lat. 2001, fol. 1r): p. 117; Bridgeman Images: pp. 35 (© Chetham's Library, Manchester (MS 6712 (A.6.89), fol. 135v)), 39 (Centre historique des Archives nationales, Paris), 40 (© Canterbury Cathedral, reproduced courtesy of the Chapter of Canterbury Cathedral), 79 (© Richard Philp, London), 107, 124 (fol. 2r), 131 (fol. 2v), 142 (fol. 3r), 146 (fol. 4r), 151 (fol. 4v), 169, 174 (© Canterbury Cathedral, reproduced courtesy of the Chapter of Canterbury Cathedral), 180; British Library, London: pp. 6 (Harley MS 5102, fol. 32r), 12 (Cotton MS Tiberius B V/1, fol. 56v), 48 (Cotton MS Claudius D II, fol. 116r), 62 (Royal MS 20 A II, fol. 7v); Flickr: p. 33 (photo Patrick/Morio60, CC BY-SA 2.0); from W. J. Loftie, *A History of London*, vol. 1 (London, 1883): p. 17; Musée Condé, Chantilly (MS 722, fol. 345v): p. 111; Sanctuary of the Sacro Speco, Subiaco: p. 92; Trinity College, Cambridge (MS R.17.1): pp. 28 (fol. 284v), 44 (fol. 230r); Wikimedia Commons: pp. 158 (photo Sailko/Francesco Bini, CC BY-SA 4.0), 164 (photo GFreihalter, CC BY-SA 3.0).

INDEX

Page numbers in *italics* indicate illustrations